PREACHING

and the CHALLENGE of

PLURALISM

PREACHING
and the CHALLENGE of
PLURALISM

Joseph M. Webb

Chalice ❦ Press

St. Louis, Missouri

Biblical quotations, unless otherwise noted, are from the New Revised Standard Version Bible, copyright 1989, Division of Christian Education of the National Council of Churches of Christ in the USA. Used by permission.

Cover design: Michael Foley
Art direction: Elizabeth Wright
Interior design: Elizabeth Wright

This book is printed on acid-free, recycled paper.

Visit Chalice Press on the World Wide Web at
www.chalicepress.com

10 9 8 7 6 5 4 3 2 1   98 99 00 01 02 03

Library of Congress Cataloging–in–Publication Data

Webb, Joseph M., 1942–
    Preaching and the challenge of pluralism / by Joseph M. Webb.
        p.   cm.
    Includes bibliographical references and index.
    ISBN 0-8272-2952-6
    1. Preaching.   2. Multiculturalism.   3. Pluralism (Social sciences)   I. Title
BV4221.W43   1998   98–17316
251—dc21   CIP

Printed in the United States of America

Acknowledgments

My gratitude is first extended to my Claremont School of Theology faculty colleagues, both past and present. In particular, Dean Marjorie Suchocki, Burton Mack, Kathy Black, and Jack Coogan have extended grace, insight, encouragement, and fruitful discussion of the issues taken up in this book. I extend deepest gratitude as well to Prof. Robert Kysar, Bandy Professor of New Testament and Preaching at the Candler School of Theology. In response to an article that I published based on material from this book, he wrote a long and cheerful letter, setting off an extended (and ongoing) correspondence that has been profoundly instrumental in the book's publication. Jon L. Berquist, too, academic editor of Chalice Press, has with his gentle ways and keen insights helped to give this book its form and life.

Much of what is in this book I owe to two professors from long years past, both of whom were mentors during my graduate school days at the University of Illinois. One is Norman Denzin, who introduced me to symbolic interactionism as a rich sociological theory of pluralism; the other is James Carey, who introduced me to Kenneth Burke and the joys of symbolic exploration. Both are still active and energetic scholars.

In recent years, I have been privileged to look back on the singular help and assistance of many remarkable friends outside of the academy, friends who have made a crucial difference in my life, and to whom I shall always owe so much—to Sam Feldman, colleague and confidant in the struggling early days of teaching; to Jerry and Lela Adams, Christian friends who provided loving resources during the days when resources were hard to come by; to Steve Ames, persistent and gentle friend who always managed to keep track of me; and to Tom Beckner, lifelong comrade, wise prodder, and giver-of-good-advice. To each of you, thanks beyond measure.

Contents

Preface

Most preachers, along with many theologians and lay Christians, are aware that churches—their churches—as the sixties folksinger once put it, they are a-changin'. Most know very well that the way things used to be is not the way they will be in the future. As a result, these are very difficult times for people in ministry, for people who must speak in some meaningful way from the pulpit week after week. Preachers everywhere are feeling pressures to ask hard questions about the nature of ministry, about how and why it is changing. The questions are spiritual ones, in some ways; but mostly they are intellectual ones. They are questions about what we believe, and what others believe; about whether our beliefs, as Christians, are the ones that must be embraced by peoples whoever and wherever they are—which is what we have all been taught and what we have preached, usually with considerable passion. As preachers, we are all sensing, to some degree or other, that the time has come to rethink, and even reformulate, the nature of the Christian mission and the Christian gospel. As preachers, we are confronted with a new *pluralistic* world, and we are not at all sure what to do about it.

Significantly, for all the books that continue to appear about how to preach, precious few actually set out to help the preacher undertake in a constructive way the rethinking and reformulation of gospel and theology that today's emergent pluralism requires, at some point, of all who take to the pulpit. Granted, there are those who remain unshaken in their view that nothing is to change, that the Old Gospel is still the Old Gospel and so it shall ever be, that changes in the world and changes in how people struggle to live together in the world are irrelevant to preaching the faith once for all delivered to the saints. Eventually, though, most preachers do reach a crisis point, a faith-challenging point when one must seriously question whether Christian thinking and theology, even Christianity's most basic historical doctrines, really can remain the same in the future as they have been in the past. However vaguely such an awareness dawns upon us, and however resistant we may be to it, most of us sense, whether we acknowledge it openly or not, that the Old Gospel, with its "us versus them" missionizing mentality, needs to be laid to rest, once and for all. Then the questions about preaching and pluralism, particularly religious pluralism, begin.

This book attempts to confront those questions in a fundamental but constructive fashion. It is significant that the issues raised here are not often explored—perhaps they cannot be—in seminary, where the emphasis must be on a certain degree of certainty, however theoretical the cloak around that certainty may be. There, Christian mission is given form and direction, and the gospel must be as clear and unambiguous as possible. Even seminarians, though, can sense the difficulty of this, and bright professors often find ways to help them through such uncertainties. The pulpit, however, remains a problem, since one is taught that, whatever one may actually believe, the "word" that is preached must be clear and decisive. So it is most often the working preacher who faces a very practical undermining of mission and gospel; that is when new ways of thinking about and interpreting one's calling become not just important but urgent, lest one be in danger of losing heart, face—and even vocation. This book represents a call for renewed thinking about the reality of pluralism as it impacts the pulpit, not to turn one from ministry or the pulpit—not at all—but to reframe the nature of what goes on in the pulpit, and explore how it all relates to this brave new pluralistic world.

Pluralism is not an easy concept to define. In fact, the whole of this book may be seen as an extended definition of it—and an application of that definition to what one says and does in and around the pulpit. Still, however, some preliminary notes on definition are necessary to put the study into perspective. It is possible to identify three recent conceptions of pluralism from a Christian perspective. The first emerged in the 1960s and 1970s. There, the idea of pluralism emerged not so much as a discovery of other cultures, ideologies, and religions, but as a push for Christians to learn about other cultures and religions as a way of effectively evangelizing people within those cultures and religions. That was when the whole world finally became aware of "other cultures," of multiculturalism. Christians—particularly those preparing for ministries of one sort or another, whether as missionaries or not—were introduced to courses in the history of religions. This was not, though, for the purpose of appreciation, but as a tool for proselytizing to Christianity. The idea was that one could no longer assume that what others believed and practiced was irrelevant. Instead, the Christian had to appreciate the origins and backgrounds of other religious faiths, since only in that way could one "labor" more effectively "for Christ" in the world.

The 1980s, though, brought a very different perspective on the idea of pluralism. Then, it was not just that the Christian needed to understand other cultures or religions in order to "win" them to Christ; it was that the Christian gospel itself could be allowed to take on the unique features and contours of the cultures and subcultures into which it was accepted. This became known in some theological circles as contextualism. Every culture, in other words, could provide its own unique context in which the Christian gospel could be both assimilated and practiced. There could be a Korean Christianity, a Native-American Christianity, an African-American Christianity, a liberationist Christianity, and so on, each with its own distinctive mode of embodying and expressing the gospel. Christians could actually encourage other cultures to shape the gospel into indigenous thought forms and collective practices, sometimes even allowing other religions to make contributions, within limits, to the Christian gospel. This, too, was more than an appreciation of other cultures. It was a legitimation of diverse social and cultural orientations as they "embraced the gospel" in distinct, and often unexpected, ways. Clearly, this is an improvement over the first kind of pluralism, but it is pluralism that places Christianity, still, as unique among religions, as the heart of what all cultural expressions of religion ought to be. Significantly, the theory on which this study is based does not make pluralism another contextual form of Christianity; but it represents an explanatory framework for contextualism itself.

As important as these developments were, however, neither prepared the way for the view of pluralism that began to impact theological thought in the 1990s. Though its roots were earlier, as we shall see, the last decade of the twentieth century has produced a growing awareness that the multitude of the world's cultures, ideologies, and religions have their own distinct and powerful views of the transcendent, their own views of divinity, of the spirit-material encounter, of salvation and sin, of human nature and goodness, of what it means to live ethically, spiritually, and eternally. And no one, ultimately—not Christians or anyone else—has a corner on the market of correctness or truth. In such a complex milieu, even the notions of "correctness" and "truth" become no more than concepts. We live in a world of many religions, some old, some new, of which Christianity is one. So the question forces its way upon us: What right do we have as Christians to try to impose, or even coax, our religion upon those of other cultures or religions, whether they live around the world or around the corner? How might we come to accept and honor, even critically, the historically based, culturally expressed religions of others? By the same token, how do we begin to understand our own religion, our Christianity, as having the same kinds of historical and cultural limitations that all other religions have? Beyond that, how are we to understand the Bible, the "book" that, as far as Christian tradition is concerned, represents "holy scripture," the "voice of God"? How are we to grasp "our tradition" and "our book" alongside the traditions and "books" of other cultures and their religions? These are the questions of the new pluralism, a radical pluralism unlike any of the Christian pluralisms that preceded it. The questions of this pluralism are the questions of our future, and they are already finding their way into our churches. This book takes up this radical pluralism, along with its perplexing questions.

Two motivations underlie this study of pluralism for the pulpit. The first is to introduce preachers and the homiletical community to a perspective that has a long and respected tradition in social and communicative theory, one that is not only relevant but even revolutionary when it is brought to bear on preaching. Before we knew about pluralism, the scholars and students of this perspective were studying pluralism within the great microcosm of Chicago at the turn into the twentieth century; in our opening chapter, we will briefly trace the history of the perspective. It has come to be called symbolic interactionism, and we will not hesitate to so name it here. The first half of this book will provide an overview of its major concepts and ideas, applying them at every stage to the process of preaching. As will become clear, it is a theory of how pluralism works, both at a micro (i.e., interpersonal) and a macro (i.e., collective) level; what it says about the interactions of preaching, about language, human relationship, conflict and volatility, and even, indirectly, about the Bible, about the biblical text, and even the nature of the gospel is unexpected and deeply challenging. The latter matters are taken up as the three chapters in Part II.

The second motive has to do with the emergence of what has come to be designated as "postmodernism," an odd, nondescript term which, at its most basic level, calls attention to the changes of the past few decades in *how we think* about things. As we shall see, symbolic interactionist scholars were working on, and charting, postmodern ideas long before postmodernism emerged, and this study will bring their creative work to the turmoil surrounding today's pulpit. At the heart of such postmodernism, past and present, are the dilemmas of absolutism and relativism, of truth and perception, of ambiguity and meaning, of certainty and scripture—all of which are particularly difficult and sensitive problems for the conscientious preacher. What should not be lost, however, is that what has come to be called postmodernism, however one defines or describes it, is part of a much larger dilemma facing the church and its ministry—the dilemma of pluralism. It is the dilemma of learning to value our faith, our Christianity, in a world of many faiths, each of which makes its own honorable claims to integrity and spiritual direction. Learning to preach in this kind of a world will require the best thinking and reassessment that any of us can do.

Joseph M. Webb
Claremont, California
Fall 1997

Introduction:
The Dimensions of the
"New Pluralism"

It has been almost 25 years since John B. Cobb published his ground-breaking study of pluralism, *Christ in a Pluralistic Age*.[1] It was written at a time when pluralism was very little talked about, particularly among Christian theologians. Cobb argued that Christianity could no longer adhere to its "supernaturalist and exclusivist" traditions; it could no longer deprecate other religions and struggles with the divine. Cobb proposed a reconceptualization of the idea of Christ, using that name to designate what he called the "image of creative transformation." For Cobb, to speak of Christ in this way opened the door to seeing "Christ" in numerous movements of human struggle and liberation. It also provided a means of finding the full operation and integrity of God in other religious and cultural expressions. As Cobb put it, "To pass through the history of religions and to internalize it is a necessary but not a sufficient condition of pluralism. It is necessary because only thereby is the relation of theology to its traditional sacred form sufficiently broken to allow for the appreciation and acceptance of other forms of the sacred."[2]

To grasp the complexity of Cobb's argument is much more difficult than to appreciate, as every preacher should, the courage of his words. That Cobb was far ahead of his time in 1975 is indicated by the fact that serious studies of pluralism by theologians did not begin to appear until the end of the 1980s and the early 1990s, and then only sparsely. The idea that pluralism was a matter of concern to *preachers* was simply unheard of, and, to a large extent, still is.[3] Cobb put his finger on the reason for this in

1

that pioneering study of pluralism. He pointed out that, taken seriously, pluralism undercuts the traditional doctrines of Christian uniqueness and superiority, doctrines of once-and-for-all divinity and resurrection. While theologians can struggle with this somewhat in isolation, in the pulpit it is quite a different matter. The great fear among those concerned primarily with preaching is that to give up, even slightly, the central "certainties" of the Christian tradition would be to give up the reason for preaching itself. The question, though, is whether such a fear is justified, and that is a central concern of this book. Cobb's great feat as a theologian (and, to a certain extent, as a preacher) was his willingness, not just to challenge those traditional doctrines, but to wrestle with reconstituting them for a new, pluralist world. The work that Cobb began is, by no means, finished. In fact, is a primary task that still must be taken up by those whose home is the pulpit.

So we shall begin in the "real world" where preachers live and work. Pluralism is the new situation of virtually every city of any size in the United States as well as in most corners of the world. It is the new con-figuration of people, whether one looks at a town or city itself, at its individual sections or communities, or at its local institutions, such as the church. This, in fact, is what most preachers have become acutely aware of, often painfully so. Over the past century, facilitated by the rise of instantaneous communication and near-instantaneous transportation, not only has the world shrunk, as everyone knows, but it has been reshuffled, something that we are only now beginning to appreciate.[4] It is not just that the planet has become a village; it has become a village of new strang-ers—and the strangers are different from each other in about every way imaginable. In such situations, humans of all kinds, with their fears and often aggressive defenses, are being pushed to cope with situations and with people for which we all seem to be largely unprepared.

For the first time in history, peoples of different races, ethnic origins, ideologies, cultures, and religions now live in the same cities, same neigh-borhoods, even next door to each other. Our children go to the same schools. We shop in the same stores and walk the same shopping malls. From the simplest to the most complex business interchanges, we "con-front" each other—Anglos, Mexican Americans, African Americans, Na-tive Americans, Koreans, Japanese, Vietnamese, Cambodians, Chinese, peoples from various Middle Eastern countries and cultures, as well as people from virtually every Latin American country and other Spanish-speaking cultures. Real, tangible pluralism has become the norm in the living of our daily lives. With that, though, has come an unparalleled level of apprehension and tension. Even in our churches, irrespective of denomination or theological tilt, we are struggling to cope with new forms of cultural, ethnic, and even religious diversity, something that is falling squarely on the shoulders of preachers. In some cases, we are sharing worship facilities with congregations, still usually Christian congregations, of other cultures, nationalities, and languages—"we" meet at 10; "they" meet at 12—but even this is often done with considerable tension.[5] Many of our churches, moreover, are seeing people from very different cultures and races trying to sit alongside each other in the same services; and, with all of our deepest idealistic desires for this kind of integration or that, we are far from any comfort level about these new arrangements.

From Sociological to Ideological Pluralism

This is the pluralism of sociology and demographics. But the result of this drastic sociological rearranging and reconfiguration has been the growing awareness of a second, even deeper, problem of pluralism. It is what we might describe as the ideological dimension of the sociology of pluralism. We are having to rethink our views of ourselves and each other *because* we are being forced to confront human difference in ways that have become profoundly personal and unavoidable. So we are not talking about pluralism as merely an acceptance of human diversity. We are now faced with considering the effects of that diversity on our perceptions of who we are and who others are, and how we are to relate to each other, whether culturally, ethnically, or religiously. In the latter area, the area of our Christian faith, we are pressed to raise questions about our own relation to our God and God's revelation to us, and about the relation of God to those "others," the ones who see and experience things so differently than do we, whoever "we" happen to be. This is, of course, the question that so troubled Cobb some years ago. The pressure of all this on Christians—whether theologians, preachers, or the lay faithful—is finally beginning to shake us to our very roots. What, though, is the nature of this new ideological pluralism, and where can we turn for help in coming to terms with it? Those are the two questions with which we will deal briefly in this introduction to our study of pluralism and preaching.

First, to get the "new pluralism" into a working perspective, let me tell two stories. Some years ago a crude anecdote, told in a number of different ways, made the rounds about a group of blind men who together encountered an elephant for the first time. None of them could see the elephant, so each began to touch and feel it at a different place. Naturally, each one described the elephant differently, the man clutching the tail describing the elephant in a strikingly different way than the man who encountered and described the animal's trunk. The same was true of the one who felt the elephant's broad, flat side and the one who clutched its leg. The point of the story was that each one's perception of the elephant was dependent on where one stood in relation to it.

As the story was told, though, it had much deeper and more crucial implications. For example, built into the story is the idea that, if two people both stood at the same place, if both of them had hold of the elephant's trunk, then both of them, theoretically at least, would describe the trunk in the same way. That would also be true if several blind men, standing in the same place, were able to grasp the tail or the leg of the animal. To stand "in the same place" vis-a-vis the elephant, in other words, would result in experiencing and even describing it in fundamentally the same way. The story also contends that the blindness of the men was the overriding limitation that kept them from "seeing" the object as the elephant that it was; and, whether intended or not, the story's message was that if the blindness of the men were somehow to be removed, they would all be able, finally, to "see" the elephant in its entirety, and then, presumably, describe it in the same way. Some agreement would emerge about what an elephant looked like.

The story, though, contains an even more fundamental assumption. It is that the elephant itself is the "reality" in the situation. The humans are there, of course, and so are "real," but their perceptions are secondary. It is assumed that if their varying perceptions could be corrected—i.e., if their "blindness" were somehow "cured"—then they would all come to see the elephant, the "reality," alike. The story, contrary to what we usually think, is not about the nature of perception; it is a story about the reality of the elephant and an argument for a fundamentally flawed nature of human consciousness of reality. It assumes the primacy and fixedness of the elephant, and the difficulty of knowing the "real." The story, though, does not describe the nature of understanding or perception—the nature of "reality"—as we struggle with it today. It does not describe what in this book we will call pluralism, even though many still tell the elephant story as though it did. It is not a matter of everyone having hold of the elephant at a different place, or that if we could all hold it at the same place, we would agree about our experience; nor is it a matter of our all being blinded by our cultural or social limitations, and that if we could just come to see in some clear, neutral, or objective way, then agreement over what we all "see" would somehow emerge.

The "Accident" Model of Pluralism

We need to try a different story, one about a very different view of pluralism. A severe automobile collision involving three or four vehicles—

there is some question, we will say, about how many—takes place at a busy intersection. Ten or more people at various positions around the intersection witness the collision. The people are not blind or handicapped in any way; in fact, they are all sharp, keen observers and know quite well what they saw. Their powers of observation and experience are not inhibited in any way. The police begin their investigation, which centers on interviewing each witness to the collision. Each describes in detail "what happened." To no one's surprise, the accounts are all strikingly different.[6] About the only agreement to emerge from the ten interviews is that a collision took place and that where the vehicles came to rest is where they came to rest, even though there is some disagreement about the skidding and bouncing of the vehicles. How it all happened, in what sequence, with whose fault, at what speeds, and so forth are matters about which there is virtually no witness agreement.

One or two observers are quite sure that a fourth vehicle was involved, though it must have sped away after the collision; they cannot agree, though, on what that vehicle looked like or in which direction it went. Two others agree on what a mysterious "other" vehicle looked like, but they cannot agree on what direction it came from. The issues of difference grow: about which vehicle was traveling the fastest, about which entered the intersection first, about which car spun which direction, about how certain items from some vehicle came to end up in a nearby doorway. In time, the "victims" of the collisions, including the drivers, will add their stories, and the number of accounts will grow.

So the question "What happened?" becomes a very tangled one, at best. Ten statements exist about what is assumed to be the same event, and while there are some points of overlap, the points of disagreement are far more intriguing and problematic. It quickly becomes clear that the "what happened" question cannot be answered. There is no elephant. In fact, there are a lot of objects, and the problems are in the relationships of the objects to each other, as well as in their origins and outcomes. Some of the objects, moreover, have now become quite invisible, and there is some question as to whether they existed at all. Nor is there any blindness here. There is nothing in the observers to fix, and, indeed, some of the observers were themselves participants.

When the "what happened" question is finally confronted, it can be handled in one of two or three ways. It can be answered by the authorities, in this case the police, in an "authoritative" way—i.e., based on their interviews and investigation—this is what took place, and what is written up as the "report" will be a composite, a brief distillation from the hodgepodge of what everyone said, and probably written up by someone who had nothing to do with the interviewing itself. All differences in the accounts, no matter how pronounced, will be nullified, and those "in charge" will make the decision about "what happened." It will be stamped "official," and the case will be closed.

The "what happened" question can be handled democratically. In this case, the witnesses would vote on various aspects of the collision and, by using, say, some fairly sophisticated statistical processes, one would arrive at a different kind of composite picture of the collision: on an overall vote of 7 to 3, this is what happened—majority rules. If we use the American criminal jury system as our model, we would place the witnesses together in a room with instructions not to come out until they had hammered out among themselves some unanimous understanding of what happened, leaving them to argue out their differences among themselves. That would surely give us a good picture of what happened. We might also say that certain of those who "saw" the collision were trained observers, so their accounts should weigh more than those who were not "trained." Or we might say that others who witnessed the collision had advanced university (or seminary) degrees, so their accounts of what happened should be held in higher regard than those of the less educated who also witnessed it.

Those are deeply problematic solutions to the "what happened" question, as we can readily see. Such approaches do little more than beg the question of whose account of the automobile collision is the "correct" one. We find we must beg the question, since it is an unanswerable one; there is no correct version. There are only the various perceptions of it; and the perceptions themselves take on an integrity, or a "reality," of their own. Who was standing closest to the collision when it occurred?—maybe that would help us. But several witnesses claim to have been the closest, so that, too, is problematic. Which view of the collision would be "God's view," if we can presume to ask the question like that? The answer is that such a question is not only unanswerable, but probably irrelevant, since any number of witnesses—being religious folk—could claim to be presenting God's view of it. So everything becomes soft and uncertain, or ambiguous at best. Of course a collision took place. Witnesses abound, and people got hurt. But no matter how absurd such thinking becomes, we are still left with the problem. The problem, though, is not the collision itself or any blindness on the part of the witnesses. It is the problem of human perception itself in all its complexity, and of the human interactions, disparities, and differences that arise from those perceptions.

What we have surrounding our collision scene are keen, credible witnesses who represent the dilemma of what we will call pluralism, or, in a sense, new pluralism, if one contrasts the insights of the collision model with the elephant model. For the Christian preacher, though, numerous questions are posed here for which answers are most elusive and troubling. As a way of setting this study into perspective for the pulpit, let us pose some of those questions:

Why are there so many perspectives on Christianity by those within and without, and why are the perspectives often so radically different from each other? We know, of course, about multiple denominations and faith traditions, and there are several theories about the emergence of those traditions. But the perspectives not only tend to stay firmly in place; new ones seem to come into existence with each passing year. Why, too, do different perspectives become so rigid and concretized? No matter where we stand vis-a-vis Christianity, its traditions and scriptures (the automobile collision), our beliefs about it all tend to become fixed, often passionately so. Why? How does that happen? Moreover, when that happens to multiple people looking at the same Christian "thing," then the stage is potentially set for conflict of a very keen order.

Why is it so difficult for human beings to accept, or even to cope with, the perspectives of other individuals or groups? Why do most of us tend to think that our perspective on something (i.e., Christian things?) is the "correct one," the true or right one—the one, we believe, that should work for most, if not all, other people as well? We all know that we have a perspective, a worldview that, in its overall configuration, makes sense to us; but because it makes such clear sense to us, it would, we tell ourselves, make just as much sense to everyone else, if only "they" could overcome their "blindness" and come to see things as we do. We know that variety is a good thing, but we remain vaguely convinced that in the big issues of life, death, religion, etc., uniformity would be better, and that such uniformity should grow out of our particular orientation to things.

By the same token, how is it that perspectives, once formed, undergo change? We know, of course, that things are always changing; flux is the nature of life itself. Still, one of the remarkable facts about individual and collective perspectives is how resistant they are to change. So what induces change, whether of a gradual kind or the kind that is traumatic in its suddenness? As Christians, we talk about conversion, but how does it work? What causes it? Is preaching related to it, or vice versa? Say that one of those who witnessed the collision (in our model) wanted to get another witness to change his or her account of what happened, what would have to take place for the effort to be successful? What factors would contribute to its success? Or—perhaps more telling—what, if anything, would give one person the right to try to change another's account of what he or she "saw" in the collision?

Can strikingly different, and passionate, views of the world—let us say of religion, Christianity—really co-exist with each other? Can people of different ideologies live side by side in acceptance and harmony? Can different perspectives about the meaning and nature of such things as race or heritage or living arrangements co-exist within the same family, community, or, yes, church or denomination? Can different religions co-exist in peace and harmony together, despite profoundly diverse ways of worshiping and honoring the powers of the universe?

Is it possible that other perspectives on the collision, or on religion or Christianity, have as much validity as does our own? Even asking that question, though, raises the thorny issue of the relativity of perspectives, an issue that Cobb dared to raise and one that we must continue to raise. Is there no absolute perspective, or set of perspectives? Is there not one perspective that should, indeed must, be the norm for all other perspectives? Is there not one perspective that we could all as human beings agree on? Isn't there one that might be ultimately "true" for all, regardless of ethnicity or culture or language? There simply has to be something normative to account for the collision for all—doesn't there? Without that, isn't everything lost? Won't the house come tumbling down? Have we really deteriorated to an "anything goes" world, which is another way for talking about ultimate social chaos?

So we come to Christianity, then, and to preaching. We know about the Bible, the Christian scriptures, and how they came to be. We know about the councils and the traditions, about the points of reformation and the sharp disagreements, hostilities, and violences that permeated the whole process. We know, too, about ways of thinking in the past and present, about the nature of human (and scholarly) inquiry and criticism. We know, too, about challenges to scripture and tradition from numerous groups, from liberationists and feminists, from historians and searchers for Christian origins. We know about the realities of Christian myth and how the most fundamental ideas of Christianity itself were framed by complex social and cultural forces. We know, too, about the recent rise of new evangelicalism, about charismatic and fundamentalist movements, about groups that call themselves Christian but that other Christians call sects. We are all, we assume, looking at the same thing or things. Yet from all of these understandings arise not only different perspectives on Christian theology, belief and ethic, but passionately, confrontationally different perspectives. And we have not even begun yet to add the deeply held perspectives on Christianity by those who are products of other faiths or those whose "faiths" are decidedly non-Christian.

A Communicative Theory of Preaching

What is left for preachers? What are we to think and say in the midst of all this? Do we batten down the hatches, with our own perspectives well protected, and preach our sermons with a kind of closed, defensive posture? Do we lock the doors on other Christian perspectives, taking up our swords against them, seeing them as some demonic effort to subvert and destroy our own sure perspectives? Or are there other alternatives? Can we as preachers adopt new Christian perspectives, or at least adapt our own to new times and new situations? And can we then help others grasp the importance of doing similar things? Is it possible that we could actually use our sermons to do such thinking and sharing? So where do we begin? Is there a starting point for an effort to grasp the complex workings of all this? More and more, the twentieth century has come to see the dilemma of pluralist perspectives not as a philosophical or an epistemological one primarily, but as a social and communicative one, with epistemological implications; not as a "How do we know the elephant?" dilemma, but as one that says, "Since we cannot really know, then how are we to relate to each other in our not-knowing?" Thus, it is not coincidental that the dominant new form of knowledge in this century has been communicative knowledge, arising (again not coincidentally) from the milieus of social relationship, i.e., sociology and social psychology. There is, indeed, a creative, well-grounded theory available to us, one that arose from the beginning years of the twentieth century and one, surprisingly enough, that confronted the dilemma of pluralism long before the idea of pluralism even came into general currency.

Ironically, the theory is related to, though not the same as, the philosophy out of which John Cobb carved his early studies, not just of theology, but of theology and pluralism. Cobb's "process theology" is based on the "process philosophy" of Alfred North Whitehead, a philosopher whose work appeared in the early years of the twentieth century and exerted a profound influence on the new faculty at the University of Chicago Divinity School.[7] Process theology contends, in effect, that religion is an emergent phenomenon, one that arises from the workings of the divine within human activity itself. While Whitehead dealt with theological issues, he was primarily a philosopher, and it was left to his students to adapt the philosophy to theology, which they did.

At the University of Chicago during the same era was a lively and well-known sociology department that gave form to a process social theory that can be described as the sociological counterpart to the philosophy of Whitehead. This social theory was born among an activist group of scholars who saw the radical demographic changes taking place in the city of Chicago during the latter years of the nineteenth century and set out to try to understand those changes. The process philosophy of Whitehead and the process theology of his students like Cobb were matched every step of the way, in a sense, by the process sociology of what quickly came to be known as the Chicago School of Sociology. It is this process sociology that forms the theory of pluralism—and preaching—to be outlined and explored in this study.

This sociology emerged from about 1900 through the early 1930s. Chicago, like a number of American cities of that era, had exploded not only in size but also in ethnic makeup and complexity. As a result of the vast numbers of immigrants who landed on American shores during the latter third of the nineteenth century, cities like New York, Boston, Philadelphia—and Chicago—suddenly became enormous patchwork quilts made up of numerous ethnic communities laid side by side, end on end, in nearly overlapping configurations. It was in Chicago, though, where this new multicultural, pluralist patterning caught the attention, and then the skillful study, of a group of young, aggressive sociologists, all of whom were based at the University of Chicago.[8] The "new city," made up of what they called "immigrant colonies" and "transplanted villages," became their laboratory.[9] Each of the distinct cultural communities that took root in Chicago, as Robert Park put it, "possesses a culture unmistakably not indigenous but transplanted from the Old World. The telling fact, however, is not that the immigrant colony maintains its old-world cultural organization, but that in its new environment it mediates a cultural adjustment to its new situation."[10]

In Chicago, the actual study and description of twentieth-century pluralism began in earnest, with sustained and influential work during those opening decades of the century. By 1912 The Russell Sage Foundation in New York had turned its enormous resources on the new social research that was emerging at Chicago. By the early 1920s, three of the most influential books on emerging urban society, along with the first full-blown theories of cultural pluralism, had appeared, and they set the course for the research and theory to follow. They were Park and Burgess' *An Introduction to the Science of Sociology* (1918), W. I. Thomas' *The Polish Peasant in Europe and America* (1918), and *The City*, a collection of seminal essays by Park and his associates (1925). In addition to these and other books, literally hundreds of monographs about cultural and ethnic pluralism poured out of that era and that city in the first third of this century, materials about cultural conflict and assimilation, prejudice, gangs, violence, collective behavior, and interpersonal dynamics.[11]

What emerged, too, was a particular understanding about how one went about studying pluralism. It arose from, and was used in, the hard work of the field research itself. It was based on two fundamental ideas that came to define the Chicago sociological perspective. First, it was characterized by a belief that human behavior could not be understood by standing outside it in some "objective" fashion; it could only be understood by getting into how human "actors" perceived things around them.[12] Every situation contained key factors valid only for the person whose actions were being studied. It was the idea specifically at the heart of Thomas' work on understanding adolescent behavior. "Therefore," as Maus described this mode of research, "the subjective aspects of the situation, the 'values,' must also be taken into account. In this connection, it was not enough merely to mention needs and wishes as such; attention must be paid to just what these needs and wishes really meant to the person concerned."[13] This idea stands back of everything that we will take up in the study of preaching and pluralism in this book. The question of human behavior and interaction is not "what happened," as though there is some detached, objective elephant, but what did each participant or "observer" think happened; and with that, we are back at the scene of our automobile collision.

The second characteristic of this social study was that it understood that within the pluralistic city that pressed cultures and ethnic communities together in complex patterns, a "conflict model," rather than a consensual one, was necessary to come to terms with how individuals and communities not only worked, but also did not work. In Hugh Duncan's words, "American social theory, and especially the theory that developed at the University of Chicago from 1900 to 1940, assumes a world in which change, competition, rivalry and conflict are normal."[14] This is important because the study of pluralism, at its root, is an effort to come to terms with conflict, with difference, and, in effect, to let differences be differences, to let them be "normal" and not a "problem" to be solved. It represents a search for the process of accepting, even accentuating difference, while, at the same time, learning to live richly with it and in it.

Thus, pluralistic theory began to take shape from the studies of real people living in a real world. It was theory, though, that was deeply concerned about people, people newly forced to live together, people trying to create a multicultural, multifaceted world that had never really existed before. Park often gave voice to the motivation and drive behind this research and theory: "The world of communication and of 'distances,'" he wrote at one point, "in which we all seek to maintain some sort of privacy, personal dignity, and poise, is a dynamic world, and has an order and a character quite its own. In this social and moral order, the conception each of us has of himself is limited by the conception which every other individual, in the same limited world of communication, has of himself, and of every other individual. The consequence is—and this is true of any society—every individual finds himself in a struggle for status: a struggle to preserve his personal prestige, his point of view, and his self-respect."[15] Few statements today capture the gist of the pluralistic imperative better than that one, written in 1925.

In addition to the sociologists and social researchers of the era, though, a second group of scholars also was an integral part of this University of Chicago milieu, at least one of whom was very conscious of the work of Whitehead. While not themselves sociologists, they became closely allied with them and their work. They came to call themselves social psychologists. They became the full-blown *theorists* of the Chicago social research. Foremost among them was George Herbert Mead, who taught at Chicago throughout the first third of the century, and who took note often of his affinity for, and his differences with, the writings of Whitehead.[16] It was Mead who developed the seminal social concepts and principles of the Chicago school, and his work drew on and harmonized with the field research that was going on around him. John Dewey, the educational theorist, early on joined Mead, embracing the emergent Chicago tradition. So did numerous scholars from other intellectual traditions whose paths cut through Chicago. In Duncan's words, "With the publication in 1923 of *The Meaning of Meaning* by Ogden and Richards, it soon became obvious that anthropologists, literary critics, philosophers of art and linguists were eager to embrace the sociological traditions of the Chicago school of social thought which William James had called to the attention of American students of society in 1903 and which was brought to the notice of Europeans by Ernst Cassirer in 1910."[17]

Explaining Conflict and Diversity

Until the early 1940s and the coming of the Second World War, the tradition of the Chicago School of Sociology dominated American social thought. Then, as Duncan puts it, "For reasons which must concern the historian more than the theoretician, the social and cultural contextualism of Dewey and Mead (and the Chicago school) was abandoned by American sociologists from 1940 to 1965."[18] The reasons referred to by Duncan are not as mysterious as he lets on. The Chicago school was concerned with understanding and even celebrating the fact of pluralism and cultural conflict—it was that kind of theoretical orientation—and American society near mid-century entered a wartime period of near-absolute consensus that lasted from the early 1940s through the 1950s.

Then came the decade of the 1960s; and socially, culturally, and ideologically, all hell broke loose, so to speak. Conflict became the norm. Not surprisingly, the Chicago conflict theorists of pluralism and cultural diversity were rediscovered. Mead, Park, Thomas, and many of the rest of the Chicago sociologists and theorists—by this time called "symbolic interactionists"—were reprinted and again widely read in colleges and universities. They sparked a whole new generation of researchers, again concentrating on pluralism and the dynamics of social and interpersonal diversity. During the 1960s, for example, virtually all of Mead's extensive writings and notes were reprinted and still remain widely available and studied. Much of Park's work, including the 1925 textbook on sociology, was reprinted and sprang into use again. What was called the Heritage of Sociology series was put out by the University of Chicago Press, bringing back into use numerous volumes from that tradition of the 1920s and 1930s. Thrasher's *The Gang* was republished, Thomas' *The Polish Peasant* was republished, and so on. Most important in many ways was the publication in 1967 of a comprehensive collection of articles and essays titled *Symbolic Interaction* (Allyn and Bacon), which became the new introduction to the tradition. Edited by Jerome G. Manis and Bernard N. Meltzer, it has by now gone through several editions, each one adding new studies. It is still the best single introduction to what we will call symbolic theory.

Even though the tradition came to life again, it did so with a significant twist. The revival was engineered not just by sociologists or social psychologists; it was also embraced and pushed forward by a new generation of scholars in university *communication* colleges and departments. What clicked for them, more than anything else, was that at the heart of this tradition is the study of symbolism, of human symbolicity, an idea that provided the mainspring of that initial tradition of Mead, Dewey, Park, Thomas, and the multitude of others. Hence, the name by which the tradition in its revival came to be known—symbolic interaction. From the 1960s on, this became the communicative theory of pluralism.

It is that tradition that we pick up in this book and apply to the process of preaching. It was a tradition of "postmodernism" long before postmodernism was heard of. It was the original orientation for wrestling with cultural, ethnic and even religious relativism and pluralism. It was the tradition that understood, early on, about the shift from the model of the elephant to the model of the collision and that took the dynamics and communicative complexities of the collision seriously. It was the tradition that decades ago embraced the phenomena of human and cultural differences, and that probed vigorously into its social processes and its communicative strategies.

In what follows here, relativity is confronted head–on, as John Cobb and a few other theologians sought to do two and a half decades ago, and as some others have tried to do since. As framed by symbolic interactionism, however, it is not a destructive relativity, but a realistic and constructive one. It even has, at its symbolic base, a new and provocative sense of human universalism, which we shall examine carefully later in our study. As will become clear, the roots of this book are in a unique and well-grounded tradition of social science, social science that offers a powerful critique of the nature of theology and theologizing in these pluralist times. This critique simply cannot be ignored by theologians or preachers in contemporary culture. It is against the background of this critique of theology (or theologies) that preaching itself must be reevaluated and re-worked. It is not a dead-end road, however, either theologically or homiletically; it is not that the dominoes just fall, never to be picked up. There are new ways, positive ways, to reconfigure our theological and biblical outlooks, and ways, as well, for us to learn to preach with a new blend that is both pluralistic and prophetic.

PART ONE

PREACHING
and the DYNAMICS
of DIVERSITY

1

Symbolicity:
Why We See Things Differently

It is commonplace by now to acknowledge that human beings, both individually or collectively, are different, and that human diversity is somehow to be celebrated. Saying that, however, does not in itself move us toward an understanding of pluralism and its implications for either living or preaching. To make that move, we must return to basics, to the root of human difference; and that root, according to the scholars of the symbolic interactionist tradition, lies in what they have long called the "symbol."

The usual definition given to a symbol is that it is something that stands for something else. In such a definition, the "something else" is taken to be the real thing (like the elephant), and the symbol is only a secondary thing; that is, the symbol is only an "expression" of the "real." One need not, therefore, be interested in symbols, since they are only the husks to be shucked away to get inside to the "real" stuff. Hence, for most scholars and scholarly disciplines, symbols are virtually invisible. It is this view of symbols, though, that the symbolic interactionist tradition from its beginning set out to counter. It took the symbol to be a means of *perception*, or even as the means for devising one's own perceptions, before it is a means of *expression*. From Mead, Thomas, and Park on, the "new" definition of the symbol was explored; it was also gradually picked up by other scholars, as it still continues to be. One can see this, for example, in the writing of Susanne K. Langer, particularly in her essay titled "On a New Definition of 'Symbol.'" A highly respected student of Cassirer, Langer came to realize, she says, that it was not just a matter of using symbols to convey concepts, as though the concepts (like elephants) were real and the symbols were merely vehicles for their expression. On the contrary. She came to argue that it is only with symbols, and the human ability to use symbols, that one can even have concepts; this is what she referred to as the "formulation of experience by the process of symbolization."[1] For symbolic interactionist theory, this is what gets us to the uniqueness— one might say the radical uniqueness—of the symbol. The assumption of the past, by and large, has been that the symbol itself determined what it "stood for," as though it had some kind of inherent link with an object somewhere. That, however, is not the case. The automobile accident, which provides a viable model for most human interaction and conflict, cannot even be viewed as an object or a concept.

We can be more specific, though, about the definition. What we have come to understand through the symbolic interactionist tradition is that a symbol is, or becomes, *anything*—literally anything—into which a human being *places any meaning and/or feeling:* that is its communicative, or socio-logical, definition. The symbol is an arbitrary human construct, arising from an innate constructive ability within every human being. George Herbert Mead, in fact, was the first to persuasively describe that human symbolic ability—the ability, that is, to create or construct symbolic mean-ing—as an inborn human trait. One of the clearest statements of this new definition of symbol has come from Leslie White, a cultural anthropolo-gist, also deeply influenced by symbolic interactionism. In an essay en-titled "The Symbol: The Origin and Basis of Human Behavior," he defined the symbol as anything "the value or meaning of which is bestowed upon it by those who use it. I say 'thing,'" White added, "because a symbol may have any kind of physical form; it may have the form of a material object, a color, a sound, an odor, a motion of an object, a taste." Then:

> The meaning, or value, of a symbol is in no instance derived from or determined by properties intrinsic in its physical form: the color appropriate to mourning may be yellow, green, or any other color; purple need not be the color of royalty; among the Manchu rulers of China it was yellow. The meaning of the word "see" is not intrin-sic in its phonetic (or pictorial) properties. "Biting one's thumb at" ('Do you bite your thumb at us, sir?'—Romeo and Juliet, Act I, Scene I) someone might mean anything. The meanings of symbols are derived from and determined by the organisms who use them; meaning is bestowed by human organisms upon physical things or events which thereupon become symbols.[2]

Beginning with George Herbert Mead, symbolic interactionism has contended that humans are born with a *symbolic* ability and that, once that ability kicks in, the unique human being emerges. The symbol, in other words, is the basic ingredient of human consciousness. Ernst Cassirer, the German philosopher influenced by Mead, has pointed out that scholars in virtually every discipline over the past fifty years have come to accept the fact that human symbolicity is the key to deciphering virtually all forms of human activity, both in its cooperative and conflicting senses. Humans, he said, have "discovered" a "new method of adapting" themselves to their environment. "Between the receptor system and the effector system, which are to be found in all animal species," there is now "a third link which we may describe as the symbolic system. This new acquisition transforms the whole of human life." As compared with the other animals, humans live not merely in a broader reality; they live "in a new dimension of reality....No longer in a merely physical universe, (humans) live in a symbolic universe."[3] There is no way to understand, in other words, who we are or why we behave as we do, either individually or collectively, without coming to grips with the symbolic water in which we all swim. We are symbolic creatures. We appear to be born with symbolic abilities; and while there are some exceptions, virtually all of our dealings with each other are done with, and only with, symbols. This is not easy for us to grasp, since the process tends to be relatively invisible to us. Kenneth Burke has put it this way:

> Can we bring ourselves to realize just how overwhelmingly much of what we mean by "reality" has been built up for us through nothing but our symbol systems? Take away our books, and what little do we know about history, biography, or even something so "down to earth" as the relative position of seas and continents? What is our "reality" for today (beyond the paper-thin line of our own particular lives) but all this clutter of symbols about the past combined with whatever things we know mainly through maps, magazines, newspapers and the like about the present? In school, as we go from class to class, students turn from one idiom to another. The various courses in the curriculum are in effect so many different terminologies. And however important to us is the tiny sliver of reality each of us has experienced firsthand, the whole overall "picture" is but a construct of our symbol systems.[4]

What is unique about the understanding of the symbol is that it locates "reality" in a symbolic world rather than in a material one. We are surrounded by a world of "things," of course—objects, settings, other people, places—and, in a sense, that material world is real: we bump into it all the time. Elephants, we might say, do exist. Yet *how* we experience that material world, including ourselves and others together in it, is a product of the other, "non-material," world, i.e., the symbolic one. Here is where we make our move to the complex and gritty interactionist world of the automobile accident, the pluralist encounters of human ambiguity and disagreement. The symbolic interactionist perspective is based on the contention that, as important as the material world is, the *determinative* one for virtually all human interactions, along with their patterns of culture and communication, is the world of symbol: that is Burke's point. Hence, the truly "real" world of human life is that symbolic world. It is the difference, again, between the blind men trying to grasp the "reality" of the physical elephant and the host of very astute individuals trying to come to terms with each other over "what happened" in the automobile accident.

The Reality of Symbols

Symbols, in other words, are themselves "real," as real as dirt, grass, buildings, and any other "objects" that one might specify. In many, if not most, cases, symbols are the only reality that we have, which is the point that Burke emphasizes, and which the auto accident underscores. This does not mean that our physical surroundings or circumstances are not important, or that they play no role in shaping who and what we are, both individually and culturally. In fact, those material circumstances or surroundings provide the backdrop against which we carry out our lives; they also provide, at least in some cases, the settings in which we are pressed to devise certain kinds of symbolic realities rather than others. In cold environments, for example, one finds complex symbols relating to coldness and the dilemmas of coping with it; in warm climates, symbol systems stressing the circumstances of warmth will be featured. However—and this is the key—all cold symbol systems are not alike, since the particular climate does not dictate what the symbols themselves will be. The same may be said about situations of impoverishment, or circumstances of oppression. While the setting may affect the nature of the symbols, it does not provide them. Certain kinds of symbols may arise in certain situations and circumstances, but there are, from this perspective, no universal symbols.

A symbol may, in fact, be held by one person as a very private symbol, in a sense. It can be given any meaning or feeling that one wishes; and someone else, one might say, would not understand even if one were to try to explain. The majority of our symbols, however, are learned ones; we have picked them up from the culture in which we were reared, or, more specifically, from the subgroups of a particular culture. The meanings and feelings invested in symbols by that culture, or those groups, became the meanings and feelings that we, in turn, invest—at least initially—in those same symbols. While Mead understood the possibility of individual or even private symbols, he was concerned with the symbols we learn, ones that he called "significant symbols," meaning those into which we place the same meanings and feelings that others around us (and before us) have placed into them.[5] These symbols make possible human socialization; with these symbols we become members of a community and the groups within that cultural community. However, the symbols we learn do not become "our" symbols individually until we, in turn, invest our *own* meanings into them, making them "ours." And no two individuals, even in the same familial or cultural setting, ever place exactly the same meanings or feelings into what we might take to be a "common" community symbol. Here, in fact, is the root out of which our entire grasp of pluralism, from its smallest to its largest senses, will grow.

A point is being made here, though, that requires elaboration and emphasis, if we are to see the full uniqueness of this conception of the symbol and its role in human communication. In symbolic interactionist theory, every symbol is composed of two intermingled ingredients. One is its cognitive dimension, or "content," its dictionary or explanatory meaning; the other is its emotional or feeling dimension. This is important, not just for our understanding of symbolism, but because of what is often done with language when it is *not* treated as part of a larger symbolic complex. Often—as in semantic theory, for example—it is believed that there are two kinds of language: one that is emotion or value-free, and one that is emotional. The idea that has arisen around this view, originally devised by Alfred Korzybski in his 1933 book *Science and Sanity*, is that value-free language is ideal language, while emotionally charged language is dangerous and should be gotten rid of.[6] Language, in other words, can be made "objective," with human emotion and involvement actually removed from it; then, it is argued, words can convey pure or unadulterated meaning, as it were.

From their beginnings, symbolic interactionists have held that language, like all symbolism, is just too complicated for such a view. Kenneth Burke, though, more than any scholar working in the symbolic tradition, has explicitly contended against the idea of an emotion-free language.[7] For Burke and the interactionists, all language is, by its symbolic nature, "poetic," by which Burke means that words contain not only some degree of emotional charge, but emotion that, since it is either negative or positive, sets up an entire attitude within the word or concept itself.[8] While Burke acknowledges that one can, conceivably, remove all emotion from a term here or there, to do so, he says, is to violate the inherent nature of language. (In a later chapter, we shall examine more fully Burke's symbolic view of language.) In short, though, words are symbols, and, as such—like all symbols—emotion can be, and is, ladled into them by those who use them. It is the nature of the symbol itself. The point is that every symbol, including every word, has within it a mix of cognitive meaning and emotional charge. And when a child, or someone of any age, learns a symbol for a verbal sound (i.e., a word, a language) or for a person or a place, that one learns both elements—the meaning and the emotion, with its implicit, complex attitude or viewpoint intact.

Signs, Symbols and Consciousness

Two other elements about the symbol, and human symbolicity, are important from the standpoint of the symbolic interactionist tradition. The first is the need to distinguish between a symbol and what is often called a sign. Even though this distinction was implicit from the beginning of this tradition, Leslie White, the cultural anthropologist, gave it its most succinct formulation.[9] A sign, he says, is a "sensory" device, something that, when present, can prompt a "conditioned" behavior for most any kind of "animal," even a human one. It usually arises as a "learned associational response," one which inevitably requires the uses of the senses in order to be activated, Pavlovian-style. The sound of a door slamming can cause a dog to rush to the door from anywhere in the house, if the dog has learned that the slamming door means a trip outside. The rattling of a box of cat food can bring the cats running, if they have become used to being fed at such a sound. A flashing red light in the middle of nowhere can cause a car driver to come to a stop, if the driver has been well conditioned to associate danger with that flashing light. Those are signs; they are used, as White says, to "indicate" the "presence" of something, whether activity or food or danger, either to an animal or a human being.

Symbols, however, are different, and for the symbolic interactionist tradition, they mark the movement from "animal" to "human" behavior, which signs do not. While signs are used to prompt the senses, signaling something's actual *presence*, symbols are used to conceptualize something, as White says, in its absence. A car horn blaring, for example, tells one that a car is nearby, but the uttering of an abstract noise like the word "car" conjures up in one's head the picture of an object that may be nowhere around—this is, if the abstract noise represents one's own language. What it conjures up is both its "picture," or meaning, and the emotion, negative or positive, that one has come to invest in that particular sound or picture. Signs, in other words, cannot solve problems. They may serve to provide shorthand ways to do things or engage in regular behavior with a minimum of effort or thought; they may also serve, in some ways, to protect or aid us in cooperative activity. But they do not lend themselves to the *conceptualizations* that enable human beings to engage in creative, problem-solving activity; only symbols can make that possible. Only symbols, as Mead put it, enable us to devise ways of "visualizing" or "constructing" behavior, including novel behavior. Burke at one point describes the same situation like this:

> I remember one day at college when, on entering my philosophy class, I found all blinds up and the windows open from the top, while a bird kept flying nervously about the ceiling. The windows were high, they extended almost to the ceiling; yet the bird kept trying to escape by batting against the ceiling rather than dipping down and flying out one of the open windows. While it kept circling helplessly over our heads, the instructor explained that this was an example of a 'tropism.' This particular bird's instinct was to escape by flying up, he said; hence it ignored the easy exit through the windows. But how different things would be if the bird could speak and we could speak his language. What a simple statement would have served to solve his problem. "Fly down a foot or so, and out one of those windows."[10]

The second implication about symbolism, however, that has its origin in this tradition is that the symbolic process itself "creates," as it were, human awareness or consciousness. It is not language that gives rise to the conscious mind, as important as language is, but it is the emergence, un-learned, of symbolization within the human being. Cassirer and White are two who have examined this element, using, in particular, the stories of exceptional cases, such as of Helen Keller and Laura Bridgman. In an essay titled "From Animal Reactions to Human Responses," Cassirer sketched his findings like this:

> The decisive step leading from the use of signs and pantomime to the use of words, that is, of symbols, could scarcely be described in a more striking manner. What was the child's real discovery at this moment? Helen Keller had previously learned to combine a certain thing or event with a certain sign of the manual alphabet. A fixed association had been established between these things and certain tactile impressions. But a series of such associations even if they are repeated and amplified, still does not imply an understanding of

what human speech is and means. In order to arrive at such an understanding the child had to make a new and much more significant discovery. It had to understand that *everything has a name*—that the symbolic function is not restricted to particular cases but is a principle of universal applicability which encompasses the whole field of human thought. In the case of Helen Keller this discovery came as a sudden shock....It works like an intellectual revolution. The child begins to see the world in a new light. It has learned the use of words not merely as mechanical signs or signals but as an entirely new instrument of thought. A new horizon is opened up, and henceforth the child will roam at will in this incomparably wider and freer area.

The same can be shown in the case of Laura Bridgman, though hers is a less spectacular story. Both in mental ability and in intellectual development Laura Bridgman was greatly inferior to Helen Keller....Yet in both cases the same typical elements are present. After Laura Bridgman had learned the use of the finger alphabet she, too, suddenly reached the point at which she began to understand the symbolism of human speech. In this respect we find a surprising parallelism between the two cases. 'I shall never forget,' writes Miss Drew, one of the first teachers of Laura Bridgman, 'the first meal taken after she appreciated the use of the finger-alphabet. Every article that she touched must have a name; and I was obliged to call some one to help me wait upon the other children, while she kept me busy in spelling the new words.'[11]

Even though these descriptions are set within a context of language learning, since that was clearly the most observable element of change that took place in these cases, Cassirer here readily places language back into a symbolic context to explain and elaborate the process. Cassirer, like Langer, understands very well that the range of symbol systems extends from language to art to music and on to many other forms of abstraction. As he put it:

No longer in a merely physical universe, man lives in a symbolic universe. Language, myth, art, and religion are parts of this universe. They are the varied threads which weave the symbolic net, the tangled web of human experience. All human progress in thought and experience refines upon and strengthens this net. No longer can man confront reality immediately; he cannot see it, as it were, face to face. Physical reality seems to recede in proportion as man's symbolic activity advances. Instead of dealing with the things themselves man is in a sense constantly conversing with himself. He has so enveloped himself in linguistic forms, in artistic images, in mythical symbols or religious rites that he cannot see or know anything except by the interposition of this artificial medium.[12]

It is only when we reach this point that we can begin to sort out the full impact of symbolicity, particularly as it applies to preaching and to pluralism. It is necessary, though, to pick up where Cassirer leaves us here, confronting the range of symbol systems in which we humans live, and with which we "create" our worlds, both individually and in community. Preaching is a symbolic activity, as we said at the outset, but its very complexity is that it involves profound symbol systems far beyond the verbal one itself. We have defined a symbol as anything into which anyone places some meaning and feeling or emotion; and the range of "things" available for symbolizing to every congregant sharing the sermon staggers the imagination. Moreover, every congregant comes into the preaching situation with a virtually unlimited set of meanings and feelings already in place— that is what opens the door to the sheer power of human pluralism. Later, we shall think through what happens under those preaching circumstances. First, though, we should get some sense of the range of symbol systems that, in some way, impacts our symbolic differences.

The Range of Symbol Systems

Language is, without question, our most commonly used symbol system, and we have already discussed it at length. Words are nonsense verbal noises into which we learn to place both cognitive meaning and emotional value. As we have indicated, every normal human being appears to be born with language-learning capability built in, and the learning of language is overwhelmingly "learned" by imitation. Later, grammar and the finer points of speaking and diction might be taught, but the initial language-learning itself does not take place via instruction. "Picking up a language" appears to be an innate drive, and virtually always under normal situations the language that is "picked up" is the language of those among whom one's initial development begins.[13] The point, however, is that language—words—represent a complex and crucial symbol system, in some ways the central symbol system learned by every human being. With the words that are picked up, or learned, comes a system of socially created and charged meanings and feelings that are also picked up with the words. In the very process of learning those words, though, in the acquisition of a social vocabulary, the child already begins the subtle but unmistakable process of manipulating those very words, giving them his or her own twists and charges of meaning and use.

There is considerable insight in David Buttrick's assertions about language in his monumental work, *Homiletic*. We are, as he says, "born into language," which "names the world, establishes roles and relationships and serves social functions," language which "contains social memory." We do live in language, which, to a certain extent, "shapes our understandings, our values and our convictions."[14] In fact, statements like this are made with considerable power by Kenneth Burke and others of the symbolic interactionist tradition.[15] Yet what Burke and the interactionists emphasize is that, as important as language is, it is only one dimension of the larger framework of human symbolicity. Language is *not* the basic element or component of human communication—not even in a highly verbal activity such as preaching. Instead, human language is, itself, a symbol system, one of numerous human symbols systems, some of which we shall examine shortly. It is not difficult to contend that language may be the queen of symbol systems, but even that statement, under many circumstances, is problematic; sometimes other symbol systems clearly take priority in human interaction, as we shall see.

The problem is that for preachers to become convinced that preaching is "nothing more than words" is to be blinded to the crucial fact that everyone who responds to a sermon responds to far more than the words that are spoken from the pulpit. In fact, the range of symbolizing going on within the congregation is staggering when one considers that the same process is going on in a different way from person to person in the pews. If the preacher believes, or even imagines, that everyone is attending only to his or her words, that preacher will end up with very little idea of how or why people react as they do to the sermon situation. The preacher's language, of course, is one symbol system to which congregants respond, and with which they interact; but it is *only* one, and often not even the most important one—depending on the individual doing the responding. If we are to understand the dynamics of the preaching situation itself, the dynamics of the *diversity* of the responses to the preaching—which is the beginning of an understanding of pluralism—we must develop a sense of the overall nature, not of language, but of symbolicity.

For example, people symbolize people. The fact is that everyone we know, have known or meet, we symbolize. This means that when we meet someone, we immediately "size them up"; we describe it as drawing a first impression, but it is much more complex and important than that. Granted, other related symbol systems such as dress or ornaments or bearing or other things will sometimes figure into this initial symbolization, so that if we happen to see the same man in a bowler hat going for a walk down our street at the same time each day, we will quickly come to know that man as the "walking man," or as the "funny hat" man or something like that. We will symbolize the person by a trait or a habit that is somehow persistent. He is the "joke person," since he always wants to tell one. She is the "handbag woman," since every time we see her she has a different, ornate handbag. It starts at that simple level, but it goes far beyond that. If I do not like jokes, then I will know the "joke man" but will cringe when I see him coming. If I have symbolized that bowler hat in some negative way in a growing-up experience, then I will be deeply suspicious of the "hat man" who walks down my street each day.

From the preacher's point of view, it is necessary for us to know that everyone we meet—and everyone we do not meet but who comes into a service in which we preach or lead the liturgy—immediately symbolizes us. Everything that we do to someone else, everyone else does to us. Each person sitting in front of us sees how we look, how we gesture, how we dress, our facial expressions, our sense of openness or reserve, along with a whole series of other smaller things—a person may, in fact, focus on something we are not even aware of—and place a particular meaning or emotion into us. No, he's/she's not a good preacher—did you notice that—blank; yes, a decent preacher—the way she held her hands out during the sermon, pleading-like, was very good; reminded me of that picture of Jesus I have hanging in my room. Things that may be insignificant to the preacher may shape the overall symbol of the preacher for this person or that one; and the process can be multiplied for everyone with whom we share the sermon.

We symbolize objects of all kinds, including objects of clothing and adornment, investing them with our own meanings and feelings. We do it for ourselves when we decide to "wear this today," since I am going to be seeing such-and-such. Suits and ties for men, suits for women with blouses and scarves—such "accepted" formal wear is often given specific meanings and feelings for various people, with some seeing them as positive and others as negative. Seldom is there a neutral form of dress, or objects to go with the particular style of dress. I like what she has on, but that jewelry is terrible—and there is too much of it. The suit on that man is not bad, but can you believe that red tie? That outfit she has on may be OK for last night's nightclub outing, but to come to church in? And so on.

Or one can turn it toward the preacher, and the "problem" of dress and vestments. Every piece of clothing, every object placed on the clothing or on the body *may be, or may become,* a symbol, whether negative or positive, for someone who sees it. I said "may be, or may become" since those pieces may not of themselves be a symbol for anyone, or they may be, or may become one, for just a few people, one here or one there; and even then for entirely different reasons. Moreover, one person who sees it and places meaning and feeling into it may be drawn to it and everything else as a result of it, while someone else may decide never to return to this church as a result of the meaning and feeling placed into "that thing" that the preacher is wearing. It is a complex, but deeply important, symbolic process.

Environment may become deeply symbolic as we place our own meanings and feelings on the spaces we inhabit. Whenever we enter a new setting, we symbolize it ourselves; that is, we place our own meanings and feelings on it—and usually not on it as a whole, though we can; but instead, we usually do it by focusing on one particular dimension or element of it, or another. We call to our own attention, as it were, this thing or that one; and it is something in our own formation of symbolic meaning and feeling that sets up what Mead referred to as our "attention-referencing" process. I don't like this setting because of that "thing" over there on that wall; in fact, I am deeply offended by it, so I find this an unpleasant place to be. Yes, everything else is OK, but as long as that "thing" is there where I can see it, I am very uncomfortable here. You may not notice it, but I cannot see anything else because of it. The fact is that, apart from a few basics of how we symbolize things and then generalize from those individual symbols to entire environmental "wholes," we know relatively little about how this entire process works. What we know though, is that no two people symbolize a given environment in the same way; and no two people focus on exactly the same thing in the same way in order to create their symbolizations of it. We place meanings and feelings on environments, on where we are, but they are not the same. If they are close enough to being the same, and if both (or more) are generally positive, then we will choose to be together in that environment or setting.

Everyone symbolizes the abstract sounds of voice or instrument that we call music. In a remarkable study of music in American black culture called *Urban Blues*, Charles Keil talks about a "ritualistic essence," sometimes called "soul," to capture the power of music as not only performance or even as shared performance, but as shared symbolic ritual. Keil says: "Bluesmen and preachers both provide models and orientations; both give public expression to deeply felt private emotions; both promote catharsis—the bluesman through dance, the preacher through trance; both increase feelings of solidarity, boost morale, strengthen the consensus."[16] This does not mean that all music is "soul music," but it does suggest that our symbolic feelings about music—the music that we consider "our" music, regardless of color, race, religion or culture—works at a very deep level of our feelings. Whether we are courting the person whom we love and hear a particular song in the background that becomes "our" song— a song that conjures up that "old feeling" whenever we hear it; or whether we have given every last ounce of energy and resources to graduate from school, and they are now playing the graduation march—we place extraordinarily deep emotions into music. So, in church, music is not just there—the right music must be there: it is that simple. If it is not—that is, if the music that we invest with strong meanings and emotions is not there—then we feel cheated of the experience that we expected to find. It is not "which" music; it is "our" music, whatever that might be. And the nature and extent of our derogatory comments about someone else's deeply felt music indicates the degree to which music is a critical symbol system in all of our lives.

There are other symbol systems, of course, such as action (ritual), gesture and insignia, and space and sexuality. These deserve careful awareness, too, and the reader should explore their full import. For example, the symbolism of gender as related to the church is profoundly persistent: who can stand where during the liturgy or worship? Can a woman step into the pulpit, or must she always occupy the lectern? How are the sacred spaces themselves gender-symbolized—by the preacher, by this person or that one within the congregation? May a woman stand at the table to administer the sacraments? No questions of right or wrong figure into this, because these are symbolic matters—and we learn and/or create our own symbols. We invest the relationship between woman and church with both meaning and emotion; we sum it up, for ourselves, in a complex symbol—our own symbol. Others have their symbols for the same relationship; and with that we move back and forth, as it were, between the poles of preaching and pluralism.

That, in fact, is the bottom line of this chapter. Symbols do not have universal meaning, nor, it appears, can they, whether those symbols are cultural or ideological, ethical or moral, metaphysical or religious. Meaning is not inherent in symbols, nor does symbolic meaning exist in some pure form in a sacred closet someplace. Meaning is a complex blend of cognition and feeling, either positive or negative, and it is conferred on "things"—on anything—by the people and cultures that use those "things." That is why we all see things so differently: both collectively in our cultures (and churches), and individually as "creators," we confer our own unique meanings and feelings on things, even the most common things. We are, by nature, the creators of meaning, symbolic meaning. In that, moreover, we lay the groundwork for human pluralism in all of its forms. With that we also set out the crux of the pluralistic problem—which is the difficulty, if not the impossibility, of saying whose symbolic meaning placed on (or in) a particular "thing" is right and whose is wrong. The implications of all this are still ahead of us.

2

Defining:
Why We Act in Different Ways

It is one thing to think about how differently human beings look at, or symbolize, the same thing; it is another thing, however, to focus on how differently—and often unpredictably—humans *act*, even in the same situations. Why do people behave in such diverse ways—not just people of different religions or those who practice the same religion in very different ways, but people who have grown up in the very same cultural or religious setting? But the question should be put more directly: How and why can honest, conscientious people—people honest and conscientious before their God—act in such dramatically diverse ways religiously— with each believing that he or she is following the clearly marked "will of God"?

This is the question that arises from our encounters with those of other religions of the world, with those of other Christian denominations, and even with those whom we know as dissenters within our own denominations. This question is at the very heart of contemporary pluralism. The symbolic interactionists concentrated on this question from the beginning of their work. From Mead forward, they struggled with what we might call behavioral pluralism—it is only a short jump to religious pluralism—and in doing so they devised a highly original and still deeply insightful perspective on it. In this chapter, we will explore that perspective, relating it as closely as we can to the process of the pulpit.

To appreciate fully what they did, though, it is necessary to know that the dominant communication theory for much of the twentieth century assumed that if two people stood in the same place and were confronted with the same "stimulus," they would, "all things being equal," *act* in generally the same way—and probably for the same reason. It was the elephant story in a slightly different form. It was a stimulus-response theory, one which believed that if one could understand and predict animal behavior, one could probably understand and even predict human behavior. So sure of this, in fact, were communications researchers at Yale University and other places that during the 1940s and 1950s they devised and carried out dozens upon dozens of experiments on students and other humans, searching for the "laws" of stimulus-response behavior. They were called persuasion studies, and they were aimed at controlling stimuli ("messages") and human responses in order to determine exactly what it takes for subjects to change their attitudes or opinions about something. The problem was that the researchers found themselves plunged deeper and deeper into frustration. Just when they appeared on the verge of predicting how a group of human subjects would react to a controlled stimulus, the group would not respond as the researchers had predicted.[1]

Finally, the researchers realized that they might have more luck if they knew the subject's attitude toward the stimulus before the study began, with "attitude" crudely defined as a subject's predisposition to like or dislike the stimulus "object." This led to a modification of the stimulus-response communication model in the 1950s. While this change, in a sense, renewed the enthusiasm of the researchers—a host of so-called "attitude" experiments were carried out—the predictive success ratio was not much greater than it had been with the stimulus-response experiments, and so disillusionment set in again. A few new concepts emerged, but most of them did little more than beg the question about the nature of communicative behavior. The goal of all the work was to "control" human responsive behavior, but it did not appear that human behavior was lending itself to anything resembling control.

Constructing an Ambiguous Room

What was missed through all of this communicative research was a fundamental principle that had been "discovered" and explored by the symbolic interactionists several decades earlier. That principle was that human beings *never* act on a direct one-to-one basis with any stimulus, to use the behaviorist's term. Humans beings, to put it flatly, are not good stimulus-response creatures. This is not to say that much human behavior is not learned behavior, or that humans cannot, like lower animals, be conditioned to respond to certain things in predictable ways. Nor does it mean that humans do not have certain "predispositions" in both personality and behavior, or that they do not develop habits which condition how they do certain "unthinking" things. What it means, though, is that humans have that unique symbolic gift and with it they construct definitions of virtually everything; they then act on the basis of those definitions and not on the basis of the stimulus itself. Even knowing a favorable or unfavorable attitude toward some object in itself provides relatively little ability to predict how someone will act toward that object in a given situation. Put another way, when college students who were the subjects of those persuasion studies "defined" the tests they were given as a great bore or a great joke, they had the remarkable ability to screw up their answers just for the heck of it. No wonder the sanity of the researchers was severely tested.

There are multiple levels, though, to this phenomenon that a simple model can assist us in developing. Imagine that someone constructed an unusual room in, say, an abandoned garage. That person built strange, abstract-looking objects, suspended them from the ceiling and walls and scattered them about on the floor. The objects were painted in offbeat luminous colors; the rest of the room was black, and deeply shadowed. It was lit only with strobe lights that came on automatically when someone entered the room. We discover the room and, as an experiment, we invite two people who know nothing about the room to have a look at it. Person A enters the room, which immediately springs to life. Person A quickly becomes terrified, breaks into a sweat, and goes tearing out the door. Sometime later, Person B enters the room; it comes alive exactly as it did for Person A. Person B, though, becomes fascinated, and finally, after reveling in it for some time, goes back outside looking for someone who can tell him what time the party in the room will begin; it looks like one he does not intend to miss.

Persons A and B found themselves in exactly the same situation and surroundings—bombarded by the same set of stimuli—yet they acted in and toward the room in diametrically opposite ways, one frightened and running, the other excited and drawn to what he saw as a very good time. Why did the two act so differently, when they were confronted with exactly the same thing? The "old" assumption—the stimulus-response assumption—was that they should have acted, if not alike, at least in reasonably similar ways. Yet we are not surprised that they did not. When we ask, moreover, why they acted in such different ways in response to the same environment, the answer is relatively easy, at least in a general way. It is that both of them brought something to the room with them, and whatever "that" was shaped each one's response to the room. In other words, we could easily surmise that Person A at some point in the past was subjected to a traumatic experience of some sort, perhaps of being locked in a dark basement for a prolonged period, or something like that. Therefore, when Person A entered the room, the "symbol" of that past experience, with all of its terrifying emotion attached to it, was conjured up—and the reaction to the room was a direct result of that previous "symbolic" experience. By the same token, Person B had been to at least a couple of good parties, and this new environment conjured up a symbol of some particularly good party of the past—with all of its positive emotion embodied intact. In both cases, it would take some serious inquiry, some interviewing—some psychological probing, perhaps—in order to find the particular symbolic definitions that each brought to the situation of the constructed room; but, given time, we could probably discover what those definitions were.

The Definition of the Situation

At its most fundamental behavioral level, this is the principle that was captured by the symbolic interactionists—particularly by W. I. Thomas. He argued that we act as we do in any situation, not on the basis of the situation itself, or on the basis of the "stimulus" provided by the situation, but on the basis of how we symbolically "define" that situation. Thomas formulated it like this:

> Preliminary to any self-determined act of behavior there is always a stage of examination and deliberation which we may call *the defini-*
> *tion of the situation.* And actually not only concrete acts are depen-
> dent on the definition of the situation, but gradually a whole
> life-policy and the personality of the individual himself (or herself)
> follow from a series of such definitions.[2]

The principle that emerged came to be embodied in an aphorism, also devised by Thomas: *If one defines a situation as real, it is real in its consequences.* By this view, behavior is not a product of what a situation "actually is," regardless of who devised or structured the situation. Behavior, or action, is a product of how one defines the situation in which one finds oneself. In our room above, one defined the room as terrifying and so behaved as though it were terrifying, while the other defined the room as a splendid party setting and behaved as though a good party could not help but take place here. That is the key to why people act in such different ways, even in the same situations, and even when they have seemingly emerged from very similar circumstances and environments.

In some ways, this sounds like good common sense, and yet, as virtually all students of communication know, this is one of the most misunderstood principles in human interaction, at least in practice. It grows directly from the "symbolic" groundwork of the previous chapter; i.e., the reality that shapes how people act toward themselves and toward each other is not primarily material, but it is the reality of one's own symbolic definitions. The material dimensions are important and, in some ways, can set up parameters for behavior; but they do not determine how individuals act. So, for symbolic interactionism, the goal is not to account for action itself—since all humans "act"; one cannot not act— the goal is to account for the nature and *direction* of the action, which is where the definitional process comes in. If a child defines what he discovers under the bed at night as a monster, he will act as though there were a monster under the bed, most likely calling loudly for help. If a responding parent goes into the room and removes a shirt from a doorknob, thus changing the shadow patterns under the bed, the child may be prompted to declare that the monster moved when the adult came into the room. It is not always easy, to say the least, to change someone else's definition just by insisting on one's own different definition; in fact, that seldom works. Our definitions become the complex means by which we cope with situations, whether simple and regular or multifaceted and unexpected. They become the means by which we attach ourselves to something that we encounter, or reject and back away from something that we do not understand or know how to define.

The bottom line, however, is that there is no way for us to talk about "right" definitions or "wrong" definitions, except as they may play out in what may be viewed as socially acceptable or unacceptable behaviors or actions. There are only "different" definitions, just as there are different meanings and feelings that people, whether collectively or individually, place on things which make those "things" symbols. Pluralistically, your definition of something—and hence your action toward or with it—may be different from mine, and while we each may argue that ours is the "better" or more "appropriate" definition—and appropriateness can certainly, on many occasions, be demonstrated—we are still left with our differences. What we are forced, in a sense, to do is to try to understand why one defines this thing or that situation as he or she does—knowing that the *process* by which we are each defining and acting is the same for each of us, indeed as it is for all humans acting in the world. Still, while the processes of defining may be fundamentally the same, seldom—if ever— are the definitions of anything held by two individuals alike. This is largely because of how definitions are both learned and then formed, the matter to which we now turn.

The Nature of Symbolic Creativity

So far, though, we are dealing with human definition and behavior on an elusive, but still rudimentary, level. It is necessary to raise the definitional process to its more complex human form. In the scenario we described about the construction of the strange room, another person is involved besides Persons A and B. This is Person C. It is the one who built the room in the first place. This is the person who most fully reflects the active, ongoing process of symbolic defining that, to some degree, characterizes every human being—and this notion of a highly active, constantly defining—i.e., creating—human being is at the very heart of the vision within symbolic interactionist theory. This means that one collects or learns symbols virtually from the beginning of one's life, as we suggested in the previous chapter,[3] and from those symbols, which rapidly accumulate, one constantly shapes and reshapes one's own definitions of everything; and with those definitions one forms the ongoing, unfolding track of one's life. Everyone does this, of course, in continuous interaction with other people in a myriad of circumstances and situations.

Life, in short, is a continuous definitional stream, since most of one's days are made up of an emergent series of behavioral decisions and actions. One draws on one's past symbols, gives them a twist of unique meaning, boils some new emotion into them, merges them with other already charged symbols, from past or present, and then acts on the basis of that symbolic "summing up." Sometimes this is done quickly, as occasionally it must be; other times, it is done slowly, more deliberately. One writes a letter with care, taking pains to define, at least within oneself, what the letter is for and how it should be worded. It is usually the way one prepares a sermon. One defines, and on the basis of that definition, one frames an action—something that will be said, or done; and does so in one particular way rather than in the dozen or so other ways in which the same situation could be met. Ironically, even when two or more individuals appear to learn a definition in an identical way, those definitions are never "processed" or internally defined in the same way by those individuals; this is because every individual who assimilates a definition must, in turn, reframe that definition or bit of information within his or her own previous symbolic mix.

One of the major concerns of the early interactionists like Thomas was what happened to symbol and definitional learning when "established" familial and social units broke down. How, in other words, do people, particularly young people, deal with crumbling definitions, and where do they turn in order to find help in framing new definitions from "outside" sources? As we indicated at the outset of this study, it is this concern with symbolic conflict and change that makes this theoretical tradition so important. Moreover, symbolic definitions of every type and shape are everywhere, readily available from the media, from emergent authorities (or anti-authorities) and even from new acquaintances, new peers. They can be assimilated accidentally or inadvertently, as in some traumatic experience, or they can be experienced intentionally, as when someone sees something that one defines as exciting and appealing. They are assimilated by exposure to new forms of experience, new groups, and new surroundings. Everywhere, they are learned and then redefined, with full meaning and emotion reconfigured, but still intact.[4] Human difference is the norm; human diversity is the nature of human behavior and action itself.

The crucial question here is not so much where our definitions come from, since what we "collect" in our growing up are not always, or even usually, ready-made definitions, but symbolic materials from which we, in turn, construct our own definitions. The question, instead, is *how* do we construct the definitions which are virtually always unique, the definitions upon which each of us decides to act. What, in other words, goes on "under the surface" of an individual, even while one appears to be perfectly at ease and even quiet? For preachers, this is a particularly important question, since the sermon situation appears on its surface to be a monologue, with the preacher active and the congregants numbingly passive. What the preacher sees as he or she looks out over a congregation is a collection of iceberg tips, but what the preacher does not see, even as the act of preaching goes on, is the lively and unpredictable activity of definition-making and sorting that is going on "under the surface" of every participant, however passive or inattentive each may appear to be.[5]

This is where the remarkable process of "mind" comes into play—and it is nowhere more thoroughly probed as a social and creative phenomenon than in symbolic interactionist theory. The concept of "mind" that originated with Mead has had an extraordinary influence.[6] It was Mead who initially argued that "mind" is not the equivalent of the human brain. The brain is an object made up of tissue and chemicals, but the mind represents a "process," something that does not exist per se, but something that happens. As William Lewis Troyer put it in an article on Mead's theory of mind, "Brains are necessary to the emergence of mind, but brains, per se, do not make mind. It is society—social interaction—using brains, which makes mind. Intelligent human behavior is 'essentially and fundamentally social'"; and then Troyer quotes Mead: "(Mind) involves and presupposes an ever on-going social life-process; and…the unity of that on-going social process—or any one of its component acts—is irreducible, and in particular cannot be adequately analyzed simply into a number of discrete nerve elements"—the latter referring to the way in which behaviorism was, and to a certain extent, still is, trying to grasp the nature of human cognition. Troyer's conclusion is that, on the basis of Mead's insight, "the psychologist should study social relations and social behavior primarily, rather than physiology" in order to know what mind is and how it functions.[7]

Years later, Leslie White, the anthropologist, would affirm this in his essay "Mind is Minding." Said White:

> To return to our starting-point: what is mind? How can a mind have a body? The solution: mind is minding, the reacting of an organism as a whole, as a coherent unit (as distinguished from the reacting of parts of the organism with reference to other parts). Mind is a function of the body. The "organ" of the mind is the entire organism functioning as a unit. Mind is to body as cutting is to a knife.[8]

The revolutionary nature of this insight cannot be exaggerated. As we noted earlier, it was this same idea that was discussed in a philosophical way—at about the same time—by Alfred North Whitehead, whose work has become the basis for what we now call "process" philosophy and "process" theology. The mind is not a "thing," but a dynamic process located, if we must locate it, in the head of every human being. The question, though, is: what is going on in the head that we call "minding" or "thinking"?

What Mead devised was essentially a metaphor for conceiving of the "minding" process.[9] His argument was that what takes place in the overt, external interaction between two or more people in conversation is precisely what goes on *within* one's head when one thinks; Kenneth Burke would later refer to this as the "internalization of objective relationship." Mead said that humans have an innate ability to "talk to themselves" just as they talk to others; so he termed the process of thinking an "internal conversation." People talk to themselves, that is, not in some abnormal sense, but in order to weigh multiple definitions or points of view and out of those multiple viewpoints to create "original" definitions as a basis for one's own actions and behaviors.

The child does this early by learning to speak aloud for multiple characters in play. My son, an only child, could be playing alone in his room, and yet if one were to stand outside his door and listen one would swear that there were several people in the room. He was the "voice of" all of the characters in play, carrying on a full, if ragged, conversation. Mead called this the "empathy" stage of child development, the stage during which the child learns to "take the role of" others—the "others" to whom the child has listened. This is the child's innate and even crude way of speaking aloud for all the "parts." It was Mead who first spoke, in this context, of what he called "role-playing." As the child matures, the process becomes well developed, and the "parts," each with its own "voice," are taken into the head and the "conversation" that was external is made internal. Also learned during this "empathy" stage, Mead argued, is what he called the "reflexive" process; this is the process of becoming an "object" to oneself, just as one is an "object" to others. One can treat oneself in the third person just as one treats others in the third person. The child's voice and character, in other words, become one more voice and character in the "group conversation."

In Mead's metaphor, all of the "voices" that one hears in any particular internal conversation are voices that one has encountered, voices that one knows, voices that have impinged on one at some time or other. Many of them are personal and close by, though physical presence may be gone. Others are social voices, voices of various authorities or authority figures, voices from religious or ideological sources, the voice from, say, a magazine article, a book, or a television program that planted an idea. The voices can come from anywhere, and they can be admitted to or kept out of one's internal conversation; usually, one has that symbolic control. When something must be done, when a decision must be made, when something is pressing, then the voices within one's head can carry on a vigorous conversation, trying to create a definition of what is going on in order to act, to decide, to "deal with" the problematic situation.

At the same time, the "voice" that one believes to be "one's own"— though it is always a constructed composite—has a critical part to play in the internal conversation, even though the "other voices" may talk back to it and even overwhelm it. Still, one's own voice Mead called the "impulsive" voice, not in the sense that it is out of control, but in the sense that one seeks intuitively, if not overtly, to be "different" from the expectations of others. One wants to be unique, creative. And in one's head, the voices are all given their sophisticated hearing; and whereas for the child they were all spoken aloud, as in play, now the voices, more honed and understood, are called up inside one's head, *not aloud, but in silence*. The silence, however, is deceptive. The head is alive with voices, contrary voices, voices that press to be taken into account, including what one hears as one's own voice; it is not always the strongest voice, by any means, but it is one that, on occasion, determines to "take control" of the situation, silencing the other voices and deciding to do "what I want to do, no matter what everybody else thinks."

This process of "internal conversation," of thinking, of weighing things inside our heads, to ourselves, applies to small and big things alike. Nor is there any time that it is probably not going on to some extent, even when we sleep. We talk to ourselves in getting dressed in the morning, conjuring up and listening to, or even arguing in advance with, the voices we anticipate that day. We talk to ourselves on the way to work with the car radio on, the radio voices becoming just additional voices in our internal dialogue. At work or wherever, we read something—an article, a book chapter, a memorandum, and silently, though often vigorously, we converse with what we are reading; there are the voices in our heads, and the words on the page are one more voice now in our "conversation"; we talk to the words on the page, and other voices in our heads talk to them while we, in a sense, listen, and those other voices then talk to us, too, about what we are "reading"; and all the time we talk back—silently—to all the voices. It is complex, but everyone recognizes the process.

The Preacher-Congregation Interaction

This is the same process through which every preacher goes in preparing a sermon. The process of "thinking," of talking with oneself, of problem-solving, of plan-making, of hearing a multitude of voices and listening in on, and being part of, their debating, their haggling, about whether I should say this or that, about how to make sense of this, about who will be offended if I actually come right out with that. Like this: "This text—it makes no sense. What in the world am I going to do with it? I can't preach this; I am not sure how to take it. Well, maybe I can handle it OK if I drop out that concept, or at least refashion it in some way...." It is our thinking, mulling, conversing internally.

More importantly, this is also the process through which every congregant goes *as the sermon itself is preached*. The faces may be smiling, or at least pleasant, and everyone sits in silence; for all appearances, those gathered at this point play passive roles. But that is precisely what they are not, at least as far as symbolic interactionism is concerned. Within every person in every pew, a vigorous "internal conversation" is taking place, except this time it is the preacher's voice that is "permitted" to be one of the voices "admitted" to the conversation. And many different voices are also allowed into the "silent" conversation in the head of one who is merely "listening" to a sermon on the subject, say, of preparing for one's future. Congregant: "So that's the text for today? Why did you have to pick that text for this week? It has the word 'heaven' in it. I suppose you're going to try to tell me that there is no real heaven, that it all means something else. Look. My grandmother—she raised me, she took care of me, she gave up everything, she suffered a long time—my grandmother has only been gone for a year; in fact, a year last Wednesday. Has it been that long? Boy, do I miss her. And I know she is in heaven."—The sermon, which is not about heaven, is continuing; and so is the ongoing stream of consciousness within the congregant—"I'm sitting here now because my grandmother took me to church—not this one, but, which one was it?—and just before she died, she asked me, Please, start going to church again. And look at me, here I am. And my kids—look at those two; neither one of them wants to be here, and yet they are cooperative. She's O.K., but I'm sure worried about him"—The sermon turns to a grandmother story—"Your grandmother?"—the internal conversation asks the preacher; the preacher's words are again a part of the ongoing "internal conversation" for this particular person—"Your grandmother was like that, too? How do you remember her?" The person listens carefully, trying to suspend a bit the internal voices so that the external one can be heard—"I like what you're saying. Our grandmothers were alike...."

On and on again. It is not that this congregant was not paying attention to the preacher, or that the preacher was having difficulty holding attention; not at all. Nor was it that the listener was "drifting" during the sermon. This is the normal process of listening to someone speaking. One doesn't drift; one "creates" within oneself as part of the interaction itself. It is a remarkable process, one that is simply not well understood. It is internal dialogue at full bore, unrelenting; and it is not the exception. It is the rule. This is the kind of thing that is going on in the head of every participant in the sermon process.

This is human creativity at work. It is the making of "new ideas," however subtle, by and within every participant in the preaching situation. Since every internal conversation is different for every participant at the same time, every emergent idea and feeling will be different from person to person. Everyone will go away with an extraordinarily diverse sense of "what was said" by the preacher, since everyone will have defined what was said differently; everyone will have made it a part of his or her own internal conversation in a unique and creative way. Each one will have reached a different conclusion—at least at that moment—about a particular course of action, perhaps some novel course of action, as a result of one's "conversation with oneself" during the sermon. One preaches in order to be part of that internal conversation of each congregant; one preaches to make some contribution to that hidden, silent conversation; one preaches to offer a particular definition of something, of whatever the sermon is about, to the congregants' highly active process of defining, a vigorous act taking place within the head of everyone who chooses to be part of the preacher's definitional process. This, in fact, is the playing out of human pluralism itself.

Theology as Symbolic Definition

From the preacher's perspective, some specific kinds of symbolic definitions are particularly important. First are the definitions that we call "beliefs." Belief statements are definitional statements. "I believe that there is an afterlife" is a statement that defines a way of looking at something; it defines a situation in which physical, material life comes to an end and one wishes to know what to call that "situation." One can describe it as a probability statement: I think there is a strong probability that there is an afterlife, though, of course, I have no way to know for sure whether there is or not. Others might put the probability involved in that statement much lower, meaning that their belief in an afterlife is very low, "but there is a chance, I suppose." A high probability judgment represents a "strong belief." It also represents a statement of intense "definition." My definition of what happens to someone who dies on this earth is that that person is still alive, somewhere, in some form. Religion itself is a definitional structure, usually one for coping with things that, in biblical language, are unseen.

Theological statements of whatever kind are also definitional statements, as ambiguous and abstract as they may sometimes appear to be. Different theologies represent different ways of defining situations relating to power, to God and the gods, to the supernatural, to the experience of human folly, to the ways in which humans symbolize guilt and its alleviation. Theological statements are also belief statements, symbolically constructed as ways to account for situations that are beyond material comprehension. One defines what one calls "sin," and does so in a way that provides a cohesive account for various phenomena; one defines a "sinner" in the context of that definition of sin. The theologian "thinks through" whatever is available for assimilation on the subject—from how one defines the Bible and its specific statements, from one's definition of historical events and connections, from definitions that one makes of one's own experiences. Through a detailed and sophisticated internal conversation, then, the theologian uses his or her complex symbol system to think through to what sin might be, how it might be defined, and then the theologian creates meaningful statements about the nature of sin, sinfulness, and sinners, along with, we might expect, the solution to the sin problem.

The same is true of the theologian's work on the nature of God, whether with a capital or a small "g." To affirm the existence of God, even, is a definitional statement, a definition of power in some form be-yond, let us say, human demonstration. One's definition of God may en-compass definitions of "spirit"—even calling spirit "holy" and then defining what "holy" might mean in such usage. But definitions confronting the theologian (and the preacher) extend beyond these theological matters to more down-to-earth issues that are usually referred to as ethical. Among these are definitions for "justice"—one of the most complex terms imag-inable—to "equality," to "responsibility," to "peace." At one level, these seem to be such easy notions to talk about, and yet even the slightest reflection makes clear that they are not. They are tangled concepts, terms often used—even by preachers—as abstract symbols loaded with little more than positive emotion; but defining them is another matter entirely, challenging even the best of theologians and ethicists. It should be clear, though, that for all the definitional work of the professional theologian, the preacher shares completely in the making of these religious and ethi-cal definitions. Indeed, every sermon that is preached becomes, in this primary sense, a definitional statement, a belief statement and a call to share that belief, to share that particular way of defining this particular situation or that one. It is a very realistic and practical way to define the sermon itself. Moreover, to talk about the "gospel" also represents a par-ticular way to define the Christian religion and its tradition; and the ques-tion within the sermon is not does one "preach the gospel," but what definition, or definitions, does one give to what one calls "gospel" in the sermon.

It is also important to remember here that how one acts in the world, in one's family and community, depends on how one defines these things related to religion, to theology, and to "gospel." If one defines the situa-tion of death as leading directly to an afterlife, and a much better exist-ence than this material one, that person would be expected to behave in a particular way; not necessarily in a specific way, since several specific behaviors would be possible, but in an overall way. For example, one would be expected to exhibit a sense of overt joy, even celebrate what might be seen as relief at the death of someone close, rather than show an abject grief. One would be expected to plan for and even talk (or sing?) about the anticipation of one's own death, based on such a belief/definition. In ethical matters, if one defines justice, for example, in a particular way, one would be expected to act in a manner that reflects that definition, calling one's actions "just," or the advocacy of "just behavior." If one's definition of justice is that God metes out reward and punishment in the form of material riches and deprivations, then one would be expected to act in a way that vigorously advocates and "justifies" wealth as the "plan" of God.

It is easy to see both the power and the importance of definition from this perspective. What is even more important, however, is the fact that all religions engage intensely in the process of defining the supernatural, the dimensions beyond human reach. All religions define God, or gods, along with how "god" comes to expression on earth. All religions define evil, giving it names and devising theologies of where it came from, of how and why it infects human beings and what must be done to get rid of it. All religions define ways of allocating power and status, of rewarding and punishing, whether in this life or some other. All religions devise complex ethical systems that define such things as justice, salvation, peace, and accountability. Christianity and Western thought have no exclusive claim to having defined these things in some ultimately correct, or even in some "best" way. We may talk about advances in living standards and technology, about "human rights" and "enlightenment," but such thinking usually has a hollowness to it when we stop to listen closely. We define our religion with all of its theological components; and we preach our definitions the way we do largely because of our traditions and because, in a more down-to-earth way, they seem to us to have "worked," as we define "working." We tend to do all this, in fact, not realizing nearly enough that other theologies, whether Christian or not, represent other—often useful—definitions, if not for us, at least for those whose theologies they are and historically have been.

Why do we act so differently, even in the same situations? Why do we respond so differently, even when it appears that we "agree" on something? The answer is because we configure our symbols in different ways, and, as a result, we come to define things in remarkably different ways as well. It is these very different "definitions," whatever we are defining and however subtle the differences, that lie at the root of human pluralism. But we are not finished yet. One of the statements made back in the early 1930s by Thomas, however, still must be confronted. He said that "not only concrete acts are dependent on the definition of the situation, but gradually a whole life-policy and the personality of the individual" follow from a series of such definitions. The question that remains, in other words, concerns the formation of "perspectives" which, together, form what Thomas calls the "life-policy" and personality of an individual. In other words, how does one come to frame a definition of, and an attitude toward, life itself? How does one define, or assimilate and implicitly define, "values," "norms" or "assumptions" about how one will live, work, think and "be" in the world?

What becomes very clear as we work through this symbolic interactionist perspective is that even the most holy, or hallowed—the most sacred—dimensions of our lives, both individually and collectively, are definitional constructs. We learn them, we create and re-create them with our uncanny symbolic capacities, and then those "things" define who we are, with whom we agree and disagree, and how we will live our lives, down to the most minute detail. But big questions remain. Why and how do we become "like we are?" Why do we sometimes seem so "fixed," when at other times we find ourselves changing, whether voluntarily or not? How does one come to be "religious" or "non-religious" in life and attitude? Or, how does one come to be an intensely partisan religious advocate, to the point of standing in opposition to those who see the world in a very different, albeit religious, way? These are the root questions of pluralism, the most fundamental questions about human difference and the legitimacy of perspectives. These are the kinds of questions that arise from what we have said thus far, and to which we turn in our next chapter.

3

Hub Symbols:
Why Our Differences Become
So Volatile

If pluralism were just a matter of human difference, there would be no problem associated with it. Unfortunately, there is much more to it than that. Pluralism is a problem because our differences have a way of turning into animosities, hatreds, conflicts, and violences. The headlines of bigotry, racism, civil war, church burnings, bombings, ideological savageries bombard us daily; nor are these always far-away things—they are nearby, down the street; sometimes they echo in very real ways even in our midst. Moreover, our differences are often couched in ultimate terms, with "sacred" invocations, so that we do not just fall into conflict and violence. We are prone to initiate such behaviors toward each other in the name of God or some other cosmic principle. Here, in a sense, is the dilemma of where the preacher stands: a spokesperson for God, and yet in the name of God human beings have battled and slaughtered one another for centuries. It still goes on.

What is at work in such behavior? Why, in other words, do we humans seem to be so volatile? Why do passions become inflamed? Why, in the name of our "principles," do we seem so prone to lash out at other human beings? Why do our differences, as it were, so often get out of hand? Within the symbolic interactionist tradition, concerned as it is with the dynamics of human action, lies a profound viewpoint on the volatility of human behavior, one that gives us some unique insights into the question of why we tend to treat so badly people who think and act differently

47

than we do. It is intimately related to the nature of human symbolicity, and thus its dynamic appears to be common to the human species.

This dimension of symbolic behavior and interaction was opened up most fully in the 1930s and 1940s by Kenneth Burke, whose place in the history of symbolic interactionism is a unique one—a literary person among the sociologists; later we shall examine in detail his symbolic analysis of text. Burke's 1935 book *Permanence and Change*, written in the midst of unparalleled international militaristic and economic disruption, remains a remarkable study of human perspectives, how they are formed, how they become, to a certain extent, "fixed," and how and why, in some circumstances, they shift and even reconfigure. In many ways, it is still a seminal study of human perspectives in conflict, of human beings trying to forge relationships across the enormous divides of nationalism, ethnicity, ideology, and religion. For Burke, drawing from the roots of symbolic interactionist thinking, it begins with the idea that all human beings, as symbol-formed and symbol-using creatures—are inherently compelled, virtually from birth, to construct from the symbols that they learn a cohesive symbolic structure, a framework that, within their own heads, is unified. Symbolic unity, in other words, does not come "with the territory"; it must be forged within the experience of every individual. This unity, moreover, is never the same for any two individuals, despite the similarities that come with living in community. It is this created symbolic cohesion that gives one a perspective, a specific and consistent way of defining and acting in the world.[1]

The Organizing of a Perspective

The key question, though, is How does such a perspective come into being? How are our symbols, whatever they are, organized within us? More specifically, how do we go about giving them their place within us? The answer to this most important question has already been suggested in the definition of the symbol that comes from symbolic interactionist theory. It is picked up quickly and used by Burke to flesh out his discussion of permanence and change. The core of the principle, as Burke put it, is that our symbols "affect us and our hearers by drawing upon the wells of emotion behind them."[2] Every symbol, we said earlier, has two kinds of material in it: cognitive content and emotional charge, emotion which, by its positive or negative dimension, represents not only strong feelings but also a particular point of view. What symbolic interactionists, particularly Burke, contend is that, as far as human behavior is concerned, it is the "well of emotion" within a symbol that gives the symbol its formative power. Moreover, it is this "well of emotion," this intensity of attitude embodied in the symbol, that provides the organizational principle for the formation of individual (and shared) perspectives.[3] Burke likes to talk about "hub" arrangements, so we will utilize the metaphor of the wheel or circle with its hub as a way to embody the organizational formation of the perspective. In growing up, one "learns" symbols of all kinds, acquiring with each one a cognitive and an emotive meaning. As each symbol is learned, it is taken into one's circle, one's own, unique, symbolic universe.

Since many of these symbols come at us and we assimilate them from different places, people, and settings, they may be only tangentially related to each other, if they are related at all. Many of them, in fact, can and do stand in conflict with each other. But learn them we must, even though we may, via our internal conversations about them, change either or both their cognitive or emotional meanings once we have taken them into ourselves. Still, we must arrange or find a place for them within our symbolic system; they are seldom "arranged" for us. For Burke and the interactionists, then, the principle by which we intuitively arrange them can be stated like this: The higher the emotional charge placed upon or into any symbol, the closer it will be to the hub of the wheel; conversely, the lower the emotional charge placed on that particular symbol, again whatever it is, the farther it will lie from the hub of the wheel. The key to this is not the cognitive dimension of the symbol, but its affective or emotional dimension.

Hence, we may talk about "hub symbols," those unique symbols that, by their placement within us, provide the key to human behavior in all of its often-terrifying volatility. Granted, many sociologists and psychologists have tried to describe the nature of certain pivotal symbols, symbols that play a controlling role in one's outlook and behavior, but the "model" outlined here has the advantage of being much more direct and, in a sense, more practical and usable, as far as getting at specifics of human conflict are concerned. Before we enumerate the characteristics of these "hub symbols," it should be said that every single human being has them. Some keep these symbols under tighter wraps or under more severe control than others, but there is no way, as far as I can tell, for one to say that others may have such symbols, "but I do not." Their presence in one's psychic and behavioral makeup is not related to either intellectual or educational level, or to the endless variations of personality or temperament. Such symbols are at the "heart," or the hub, of even the most erudite and articulate individual as well as the most uneducated person. The difference appears to be, as we will discuss later, in the degree to which one develops a *consciousness* of these symbols and learns to maintain control over them. But they are there in each of us, making us what, at our most emotional and volatile moments, we are. Before we are finished here we will consider how one goes about uncovering one's own hub symbol system.

The Characteristics of Hub Symbols

There are several characteristics of these hub symbols. First, these are, for each individual, the "sacred" symbols, with the word sacred used here not in any religious sense, even though such hub symbols can certainly be, and often are, religious in content. Kenneth Burke has called these symbols "God-terms" or God-symbols. These are the symbols that are invested by their holder with so much emotional charge that they become the "ultimate" symbols to that person. They are invested with full personal and collective sanctity, at least for the person who holds them at the center. Moreover, they are sacred in the sense that they *must not* and *cannot* be derogated by someone else without their holder's feeling violated in some ultimate sense. These are the symbols that are invested with, and as a result that "call up" for that individual, what we know as awe-filled emotions or feelings. These are the symbols that we often believe have come from someplace "beyond ourselves"; that is the strength of the emotion that we load into them. These can be either positive or negative feelings, with the symbols themselves standing for ultimately righteous or ultimately evil things—often as two sides of the same symbolic coin. These are symbols that an individual is ultimately "for" and ultimately "against." These are the symbols, moreover, that those who hold them seek to defend, usually literally and sometimes even in violent ways, against their desecration. Those who do desecrate, or "put down," someone else's hub symbols are, or at least can be, the object of deeply emotional negatives, sometimes (again) to the point of danger.

Second, hub symbols comprise what are generally called one's "values." The hub symbols, with their intense energy charges, *are* the values. As we have said from the outset, the symbolic interactionist point of view is that there are not values first and then we find symbols for expressing or embodying those values. The contention here is that the hub symbols, whatever they are, are the values. It is the hub symbols themselves that one "stands for." As a result, these are the symbols that hold together the rest of one's symbolic world. They provide the glue that relates, or connects, virtually every other symbol that one holds. One's symbols, in other words, take on a consistency with each other, to the point that those symbols which do not naturally fit into one's overall system are altered or even changed dramatically so that they do "fit." If the symbol "justice" is at the hub, it will be defined in a particular way and then charged with an enormous amount of positive emotional value; that symbol, then, will most likely spread its emotional "charge," whether it is negative or positive, throughout one's symbol system so that everything one talks about and acts toward will in some way be affected by that "value," that hub symbol of justice. That particular hub symbol, for that person, may not be directly matched to anyone else's hub symbol—even of the symbol "justice"—but for the one who's hub symbol it is, it will function as an ultimate value in a particular way for that person's life.

Third, hub symbols are the assumptions or the "facts" upon which one lives and works. Hub symbols do not have to be defended, even though we are usually ready to defend them. They do not have to be proven, argued for, or even examined. They just *are*, and what they stand for, the emotion that they contain, is, for the one who holds them, *self-evident*. Translated into statements, hub symbols do not represent opinions or ideas; they are not expressions or interpretations. They are "facts." They are the "truth," whether one defines that "truth" with a capital T or a small t. It is assumed by each individual that these hub symbols are "the way things are," whether they stand for transcendent or immanent things, whether they are about the nature of God, about human nature or about human relationships. Though we can, on occasion, acknowledge that our hub symbols are our beliefs, deep down we think of them not as beliefs but as a form of universal reality itself.

Finally, the hub symbols within us are the symbols that shape not only our outlooks, but what we take to be the "real" world in which we live. They shape, in other words, our identities, both as we perceive ourselves and as we labor to cause others to perceive of us. The hub symbols within us fashion, with our help, "who we are" and how we want others to know us. More than that, our hub symbols fashion our orientation to everything. They let us make sense of how we live and how we would like everyone else to live. They provide our worldview. Our perspective on life, with all of its pieces and ingredients, is a product of the configuration and content of our hub symbols.

These are the symbols, moreover, that frame virtually all of our relationships with other people, whether we know them individually, as strangers, or even as foreign people with a particular look or cultural orientation. Here our hub symbols exert their most profound effects. As a result of our hub symbols, we become bonded to certain people, and intensely repelled by others; with these symbols, we love and we hate, we are interested and curious, and we are suspicious and frightened. It is these symbols that, in fact, lead us beyond disagreements with others to intense rivalries and animosities. These are the symbols from which human volatility and conflict arise and erupt. These are the passionate symbols, possessed by every human individual, which, when poked, or stirred, or derogated, can burst into a fit of anger and fury; this, in turn, often gives rise to anger and fury in the "other person" as well. What we are describing, in fact, is one of the central marks of human interaction, ranging from annoyed separation between two people to angry outburst, erupting in a lashing out of some sort or a breakdown into tears or a pointed refusal to "ever again" keep company with that person.

When Hub Symbols Conflict

The deep injuries and the hurts that we feel, and that we inflict on each other, are invariably a result of a conflict between human hub symbol systems. For example, two people are talking in an enjoyable and animated way. Suddenly, one person changes and joy instantly turns into pain and tears. The other person in the encounter is bewildered, seeing the action of the partner. The conversation ends abruptly. What happened?—that is what the first person wants to know. The answer is that something that was said sent a sharp jab, as it were, into the hub area of the other person, and the pain was instantaneous and deep. When our hub symbols are pricked, poked, derogated, made fun of, treated flippantly—when these kinds of things take place, whether they are deliberate or not, we react to the psychic, or the emotional, pain. Our reaction may be passive, as in crying or in running away from the encounter; we may hide the pain and just become quiet and inattentive. Or, it may be very active, as in striking back in some almost instinctive way; we may shout back, "You can't talk like that," or "What gives you the right to say that!" Or one may, on occasion, actually strike back in some more violent fashion in response to what has been done. Our encounters with each other are constantly fraught with these episodes; and they cannot be explained, or understood, apart from an awareness of the hub symbol process.

Moreover, human divisions, splits, and hatred arise from overt and brutalizing clashes of individual hub symbols. One must understand what kinds of symbols most often are in our centers, our hubs. They are symbols for our religions, for races, genders, ideologies, nationalisms, and economic situations. While any symbols can be hub symbols, symbols from these areas—whether words, concepts, flags, names for roles, whatever—are heavily loaded with emotion and protected in our hubs. And when these hub symbols are derogated, lines are quickly and often furiously drawn between individuals and groups. For the feminist with feminist symbols at the hub, there is little tolerance of those who derogate feminism by using anti-feminist hub symbols. The fury of one can quickly flare into a mutual fury. For the person with hub symbols of a rigid ideological Right, to hear those symbols derogated is to respond with something that can often be described as hatred, and the lines are quickly and aggressively drawn. It is the full power of hub symbols at work.

The presence and the power of these symbols are not difficult to demonstrate. If one takes an issue like the role of women in church leadership—or, more recently, the issue of gay roles and rights in the church—hub symbols can assert themselves from every side and corner. But let me stick with the issue of women in leadership. In my own experience in the mid-1980s, while ministering to a church of about 150 regular worshipers, a woman who was an attorney and lifelong member of the church asked if she could become more involved in the church's worship; specifically, she asked to assist in distributing the Lord's supper, something that our free-church style did regularly and relatively informally. The small board of the church said yes without so much as a comment, and the next Sunday there she was with three men passing the communion elements up and down the rows of worshipers. The tension was immediate, felt even before that service was over as some refused to participate in the elements that came from her hand. By day's end on that Sunday, one-third of the congregation had quit the church. I was stunned; it was not an outbreak of hostility that I even anticipated back then. I went from house to house among the church members, and in every house the emotions were brutally intense, both for and against what had taken place. There were few, if any, neutral, I-can-take-it-or-leave-it people. "Sacred" symbols, religious and otherwise, had been called to the surface. Hub symbols had been fully activated, the kinds of symbols that divide people in hostile and often permanent ways on virtually any issue or action.

Where do we get our hub symbols? Where do they come from and how do they develop? This is a critical question if we are to understand their dynamics. We get them where we get all of our symbols: from the people and cultural settings in which we grow up. We are not born with symbols, and certainly not with hub symbols. Instead, as we saw earlier, we are born with a symbol-using ability, and, we might now add, with a "hub symbol" ability. These unique, emotionally charged symbols that all humans possess do not come to us in some mystical or spiritual way; we may, no doubt, through mystical or spiritual means enhance them in some ways, but they remain symbols nonetheless. They are acquired and formed within our lives in the same way, or ways, that we acquire and come to use all of our symbols. The only difference with these symbols is their intensely emotional character. We know, however, that we "learn" most of our hub symbols from three kinds of settings or circumstances, each of which needs some explication.

The Sources of Our Hub Symbols

First, many of our hub symbols—or the hub symbols of many persons—come from an individual's "primary" or "familial" group. This is not just parental, and sometimes it is not parental at all. It is that circle of individuals into which one is born, whether it is a tight-knit circle of parents and siblings, an extended family of some kind, or even a clan-like circle in which children are treated communally.[4] This is invariably one's initial exposure, not only to symbolism itself, but also to hub symbols. Here one encounters at a very young age the first sustained expressions of full-blown emotion. Here one encounters for the first time outbursts of emotional intensity—angers, frustrations, hostilities, often with clearly identifiable objects in view. Here one initially encounters the sustained emotional involvements in profession or religion or avocation and experiences the symbolic fabrics of those emotionally driven behaviors. It should not be surprising that children often emerge following the "footsteps" of their parents, whether professionally, religiously, ideologically, or however. The parental hub symbols become the hub symbols of the child; they are learned emotions with symbols attached. So battered children easily become batterers; children who experience the deeply emotional (i.e., hub) entanglements of parental drug use have no difficulty embracing the emotions and hub patterns of drug use themselves. Hub symbol cycles are often set up that run generationally.

A second place from which hub symbols are learned are from what social psychologists have come to call "reference groups." Reference groups are of two general kinds for all of us as we grow up. The first kind are those into which we move and to which, to some degree, we become attached. We may stay on the fringes of these groups, learning some of their symbols, but keep them relatively low in emotional content—keeping those symbols, as it were, away from our hub. For me, Scout groups were that way when I was young; I never got into them like some of my friends did, so while I learned a certain amount of Scout language and symbolic activity, it never became "important" to me. For some of my friends, Scouting became everything, a part of their "hub arrangement;" for me, though, it was other groups, like church and participatory sports. The second kind of reference groups are those that we "learn" to symbolize, in a sense, from afar. We do not join them, but we learn them as "symbolic" entities, groups that we do not like and that we want nothing whatever to do with, groups that are negative in some way. They are important to us, not because of our participation in them, but precisely because we do not want, ever, to be associated with them or anyone who is in them.

In both cases, groups—or rather the symbols we associate with those groups—become crucial to our own hub symbol formation. Let me illustrate this by indicating how the symbolic interactionist tradition has defined the group with the symbol always at the core. The view is that groups do not first exist and then form symbols that express their life and character; on the contrary, groups can only exist, or come into existence, around a central set of symbols which comprise a symbolic fabric. Say, hypothetically, that I love playing marbles and I have ever since someone taught me to play when I was young. I tried it and had fun at it, so I continued—but always alone. One day, as an adult, I let it slip that I planned to play marbles that evening at home, only to find someone next to me at work—someone that I never particularly liked—who heard me and confided that he, too, had grown up loving to play marbles. My dislike toward him immediately shifted, and I invited him over for an evening of marble-playing.

Over the course of the next several weeks, the word got around that we had some marble-playing going, and, one by one, several others asked if they could join us: they, too, had grown up with marbles. So our group began to take shape—a group that had at its core one central symbol: the joy and importance of marble-playing. As our group grew, we embellished our "symbol." In my basement, we devised a first-class marble-playing floor, complete with painted lines, practice areas, and special marble-rolling turf. We charged dues in order to pay for it all. We grew rather sophisticated in our marble-playing language: there are no marbles as such; only cats-eyes, aggies, steelies, and so on; and we expected everyone to "talk the talk." We divided into teams, with practice times allotted to each team before our regular Tuesday night play time. Our teams, one by one, began to devise modes of dressing alike, with colorful marble logos, and so on. Other teams in other towns began to emerge, and we joined with them in a kind of league.

One day I find myself in my work mode attending a business convention for my company. I am going about my usual suit-and-tie business, and sitting next to me is someone I have never met, but within the bundle of materials he is carrying is a worn copy of *Marbles Monthly*, a publication that I know very well. Despite the meeting, I slip him a note about marbles. I immediately know that I have a friend. As soon as the meeting takes a break, we will talk, probably long and intently, about marbles; and when we part we will, most likely, make plans to stay in touch.

What would happen, though, if I should wake up some morning with a cold but clear realization that marble-playing is an embarrassing activity for a grown man like me to be engaging in? It is ruining my life with the time, money, and energy it takes that I could be putting to much better use. I have, after all, been ignoring my family to play marbles; but now, by some quirk of realization, I know I must quit. I make some phone calls telling my friends that I am quitting, but I say I hope that I can still come around and that we can all still be friends. But they let me know quickly that we will not still be friends. They do not understand my decision, and they do not want me around. No, they "fire" me. The problem, in short, is that our "friendship," as intimate and intense as it has been, is based on our shared symbol system only—on our shared hub marble system. Without that, what remains is nothing that could be called a friendship. Our relationship comes to an end.

Individual and Group Hub Symbols

Such is the model, symbolic interactionist theory argues, for any human group. There will be variations on it if it is a "required" group, such as a school or work situation, and even for various kinds of "voluntary" groups, such as for recreation or religion. But the dynamics are fundamentally the same. The group arises from and is sustained by a symbolic fabric, and anyone who comes into and functions within the group must embrace, and assimilate, not only the symbols of the group but the emotional weights carried by those symbols. The point is that if one becomes deeply involved in a marble-playing group, then marbles and marble-playing become a part of that individual's hub symbol system. One can stay on the fringes, of course, and keep marbles out of one's hub, but in so doing one never becomes important to the group. When marbles are in one's hub, though, someone else cannot belittle or make fun of marble-playing or otherwise derogate it without incurring the emotional alienation, if not wrath, of the committed marble-player. Many hub symbols arise from involvements in such reference groups, whether they are athletic, hobbyist, work-oriented, or even religious.

There is a third source of hub symbols. These are the ones that arise from the traumatic episodes of one's maturation. While sometimes more difficult to identify, their place in an individual's hub can be very intense and pervasive, if more invisible. A child who sees one parent severely attack or even kill the other parent will undoubtedly frame a hub symbol, or set of hub symbols, from that trauma. A child who experiences a devastating automobile accident, or a crippling or disfiguring accident may very well turn the experience implicitly into a hub symbol. When I was barely a teenager, my friends and I enjoyed sports, particularly track and field. In order to practice various "events" in the summer, we rigged makeshift spaces and objects in our large yard, using everything from flour for starting and finishing lines to carefully set tree limbs that served for high jumping. One of the events that fascinated us was the hammer throw, and since we had no "ball and chain" we had to make one, which we did with a three-hole brick and a long piece of clothesline. By twirling it over one's head, one could sail it far out over the high peony bushes into the long vacant lot next door. It was my turn on a late Sunday afternoon to throw the "hammer" and three of my friends were the lookouts in the vacant lot, since I could not see where the thing would land. But Kenny Renner, a pesky, younger kid was out that day, and he went running across the vacant lot just as I let go of the brick. It hit Kenny in the head. He was in a coma for several weeks, though one of the happiest days of my life was the day I learned he would survive. The three-hole red brick became a hub symbol for me that day, filled with the deepest emotion over what I had done to Kenny Renner. It has, I should say, drifted out from my hub somewhat over the years; the emotion has eased, but seeing a brick can bring much of it back in a flash.

As we said about symbols themselves, anything—literally anything—can become a hub symbol for anyone; and it can be pushed or wrenched into the hub at any time in life. Moreover, every group into which we move, from our earliest experiences, is a group that has as its mainspring some set of hub symbols, like the marbles at the heart of the marble-playing group. To become enmeshed in that group is to assume, at least to some extent, that group's hub; and if that group becomes very important in one's life, then that group's hub becomes a hub symbol within the individual for whom the group is intensely important. The religious importance of this cannot be overemphasized.[5]

What we are ultimately confronted with here, though, is not just some intellectual understanding of a social-psychological phenomenon, but a sense of what this all has to do with pluralism and our responsibility to preach within a pluralistic context. We are faced, in a sense, with what preaching is for—though that is a question to which we shall return later. What we are after is pluralistic integrity in the pulpit and in our dealings with other people. Of course, preaching is and must be a persuasive activity—the process of symbol-using itself is a persuasive activity that seeks to influence the symbol-using of others—but it must not be a manipulative one. But notions of persuasion and manipulation are so vague as to be almost meaningless. So we can ask, at this point, that our preaching reflect "symbolic" or "pluralistic" integrity. This means, by and large, three things with which we may sum up this chapter, and this exposition of symbolic interactionism.

The Nature of Pluralistic Integrity

The first is that pluralistic integrity requires an awareness that what we have called hub symbols are at the core of every one of us—symbols that are "sacred," that are the embodiment of our very value systems—but they are, without exception, *symbolic constructs*. They are symbols that we have learned, have assimilated, often with heavy emotion already present within them, sometimes laden with the intense emotion that we ourselves have placed upon them. But they are *finite* symbols nonetheless. This, however, is not an easy notion to grasp, since of all of our symbols, these are the ones that we want to believe originated from "above and beyond" us. We want these symbols to be sacred precisely because they are not "our" symbols. They are God's symbols, we tell ourselves, however one might configure the symbol of God. We want these symbols to be non-opinionated symbols, non-interpretative symbols; we want these symbols to be "factual" symbols, symbols that are the way we "hold" them because they can be "held" in no other way. We want these symbols to be absolute, and yet, realistically, they are not. No matter what they are, and no matter how many individuals may, in a sense, "hold them in common," they are relative symbols and symbol systems. Still, when someone, anyone, attacks these symbols, they attack us, because, shall we say, we are these symbols, and they are us. So we must come to terms with the understanding that, despite such intensity, these are still symbols—whether held by us or someone else—and, as symbols, they are relative and limited; and they vary from person to person, even though we all seem to embrace them in the same way. Recognizing this, and dealing with it, is the beginning of a move toward pluralistic integrity.

Second, pluralistic integrity requires each one of us to develop as full an understanding as possible of what our own hub symbols actually are. This involves what can only be described as a grueling form of introspection, of searching within oneself. Over the years, I have required students to write what I call "symbolic autobiographies," a deeply valuable exercise. The question, though, is how one goes about "uncovering" one's own hub symbols. Though it is never an easy thing to do, there are three fairly well-defined steps in the process. First, one must actually identify what the hub symbols are to which one holds. The problem is that often they are deeply buried and must somehow be "dug up"; or that they are so close and visible as to be invisible. Often, too, one's hub symbols have so much emotion attached to them as to resist being directly looked at and talked about, even with oneself. So one must be intent on the task and sure that the process is worth it, which, for the preacher and theologian, it is.

My experience has been that the easiest way for one to uncover one's own hub symbols is by approaching the task negatively. That is, by asking oneself—and responding candidly—what someone might say that would cause "me" to feel great intellectual or emotional pain. I really get upset or angry when someone tells me that—and there the blank may be filled in. When they talk about race or what women shouldn't do or about laziness or obesity or about patriotism or whatever, or when they tear down the church or deny the divinity of Christ or say this or that about the Bible—I get upset and defensive. Whatever "that thing" is or "those things" are that produce that reaction reveals the presence of one's own hub symbols. With each negatively charged hub symbol is usually a positively charged one, the reverse side, as it were. What I really can get passionate or worked up about is—and again one may fill in the blank. I really get emotional when I get a chance to preach about—we can all fill in something there. Those are the hub symbols. How deeply they are actually buried within an individual, and how difficult it is to actually face what they are will vary from person to person. Our beliefs are often our hub symbols, both positively and negatively. Our religious or theological commitments are often our hub symbols. Our lifestyles, our ways of defining evil and good—all of these comprise what are often one's hub symbols. But they are there for everyone, and finding them, uncovering them, is what the preacher must do.

The second step, then, after one has a pretty good idea what one's hub symbols are, is to "track them down." That is, one must take each one, as much as one can actually single them out, and search back in one's own life and experience to determine where one "got it." Where was its source, as far as one's own individual experience is concerned? Here the idea of the "sources" that we discussed earlier becomes important. Did the high emotional charge come from a parent, from some other highly influential individual from one's childhood or youth, or from some particular experience which can be readily pinned down, as often they can? The point here is that we are usually inclined to take our own hub symbols as having come from someplace mystically beyond ourselves, even "from God"— the hub symbols have that kind of sacredness about them within us. Yet when we "track them down," we readily discover that they did not come from God, but from someplace or someone much closer, shall we say. Often, too, when we track them down we discover just how painful the experience was that created the hub symbol within us, as many therapists who deal with such things as child molestation know only too well. But learning about the finiteness of our hub symbols, whether they are our theological beliefs or religious convictions, is a crucial dimension in coming to terms with pluralism itself. One's own passionately held hub symbols are just like everyone else's passionately held hub symbols.

The third step in this awareness-building process is that one returns to one's hub symbols, then, to "take control" of them. They do not lose their emotional power, nor their ability to produce intense pain when they are attacked. What one can do, however, is to experience that pain, be aware of what it is and what caused it, and then control one's reaction to the pain itself. One need not, at that point, strike back, attacking the other person's hub symbol, which appears to be the normal human reaction. One can, in a sense, absorb the pain of a hub symbol attack without retaliation, thereby defusing an attack which, if unchecked, will usually deteriorate into a bitter severance of relationship. There is no way to explain how important this ability is, particularly for preachers. That preachers' hub symbols are often attacked and derogated goes without saying. Often, it is not even deliberate. But to control the response that one's hub symbols might, in fact, call up is to preserve encounters, and even relationships, that may be seriously jeopardized. To hold in abeyance one's overt response to a hub symbol attack is often a way to preserve a dialogue that otherwise would break down.

Having described, though, how one goes about "discovering" one's own hub symbols, there is another dimension to what we have called pluralistic integrity related to these hub symbols. It is that pluralistic integrity requires an awareness of what is going on in another person when he or she erupts with anger, defensiveness, or hostility. It is not just a matter of holding one's own overt response under control; it is also a matter of knowing that deeply emotional outbursts from someone else, in whatever form and in whatever context, are always "made" of the same thing. A hub symbol of some kind has been seriously challenged, even wounded. The reaction to that is invariably a striking out and a striking back. One may not, in fact, know what the hub symbol is; it may even be disguised in some way, since we all know how to do that. But the hub symbol is there, someplace, and, in time and with careful listening and even some question-asking, one can usually discover what it is. Again, though, it is not just a matter of knowing something. It is that, *if* one knows that, one is able, again, not to respond in kind, even though that is usually what the impulse would summon one to do.

How do we grasp and deal with our differences, with human difference? That is the pluralistic question. It begins in dealing with ourselves, in self-understanding. It begins also in coming to terms with the dynamics of human diversity—with diversity, that is, in its most passionate and emotional forms. We have tried to explore some of the dynamics of those diversities in this chapter. What, though, are the implications of this entire symbolic perspective for the ministry and, in particular, the process of preaching? In the second half of this book, we turn specifically to some of those implications. It will not be easy going. The challenges to our accepted ways of thinking and acting are everywhere, but we shall try to confront them meaningfully and creatively.

PART TWO

IMPLICATIONS
for PREACHING
PLURALISTICALLY

4

Pluralism and the Bible: Preaching and the Symbolism of the Book

Christianity is a pluralist religion, albeit not a happy one. Most Christians would like for "other" Christians to be like what they are; enormous energies and resources, in fact, are spent in trying to proselytize among the myriad Christian traditions and denominations. Ironically, the thing that is the most emotionally divisive barrier that separates Christians at the beginning of the twenty-first century is seldom addressed, and that is the Bible—not the Bible as the handy repository of the church's texts for polity and preaching, but the Bible as Bible; the Bible, that is, as Christianity's central symbol. For virtually all Christians, the Bible is not just another book; it is "the book," an object into which intense and virtually unshakable emotions are placed, the Bible as every Christian's hub symbol. So a study of symbolism and pluralism as both relate to Christianity must begin there—with the Bible as symbol.

People define, or symbolize, the Bible in strikingly different ways, usually investing their definitions with the most intense emotional charges. Scholars, too, and theologians define the Bible in profoundly different ways as well; and also with intense emotions. Until we grasp the spectrum of deeply held emotional definitions of the Bible, we will make little headway in coming to terms with the pluralistic world of the Christian religion. The fact is, though, that until recently—i.e., the last century and a half—Christians of whatever stripe were in remarkable agreement over how the Bible was to be defined. That has all changed now; and the proliferation of definitions of it seems to be accelerating. Those who preach must learn not only to confront the different definitions, but also how to deal with them in the pulpit.

Describing the definition is something of a problem. It is best solved by seeing the emergence of the pluralist views of the Bible as a historical evolution, one that has its roots in both the Protestant Reformation and the secular Enlightenment. It is well known that when Protestantism forced itself from the belly of the Roman Catholic Church, the baggage of doctrinal infallibility that had been borne on the shoulders of the papacy was transferred to the Bible. Protestantism became not the religion of the ring, but the religion of the book. While biblical and doctrinal interpretations differed from reformer to reformer, giving rise to the various well-defined Protestant denominations, the various emergent strands were united in collectively placing a hold around the book. The Bible, however it came into being, was taken to be the Word of God. It became the symbol for God's voice. The power and mystery of the book seemed so much clearer and more trustworthy than the pronouncements of a papal personage. The Bible was intensely studied. Its infallibility was seldom argued for; it came to be assumed. Its words were God's words, and even though the various denominations heard those words differently, with different meanings and emphases, what was almost universally accepted was a reverence for the words as divine utterances from the heart and mind of God. Even the long years of the Enlightenment, which emerged from the sixteenth century with Protestantism and opened the door into the world of scientific thought, could not deter the profound infatuation with the Bible as Bible.

The Enlightenment, though, gave birth to a different orientation to life, one based in a sense of history. It was not until the middle of the nineteenth century that the full sense of the historical as both a process and an object of study began to impact Protestantism. When it did, however, a new view of—i.e., symbol for—the Bible quickly took shape, not to replace the "original" one, but to challenge its hegemony. In Europe, biblical scholars pushed back the edges of historical critical thinking as they began to apply it systematically to the Bible; they had begun the arduous task of uncovering the Bible's own complex historical roots. What became clear was that the Bible, too, had a history. It was composed of bits and pieces that, to some extent, could be tracked, pieces of legend and oral tradition, fragments of mythic retelling, drawn from various existing traditions and then embellished and fashioned around the figure and image of Jesus, bits of imaginative fiction and color. From all the pieces, a document was drafted from within this community or that one, for polemic or propaganda or instruction. The collection and collation processes were, themselves, complex in their historical evolutions. It took councils, gathering and arguing, to make decisions, rejecting many odd, if similar, pieces, while selecting a few to be placed into "sanctioned" circulation. The story of it all has, by now, been told a thousand times.

Same Words, Different Definitions

The rise of biblical historicism set off a simmering but brutal battle. From the mid-nineteenth through the opening years of the twentieth century, it was largely an intellectual battle, a scholar's battle. It amounted to a contest over how to "define" the Bible. Was the Bible to be an ahistorical book, as it had been for centuries? Or was the Bible a historical book, subject to all the vicissitudes of historical composition and compilation? Was the Bible a book which embodied clear, verbal "directives" of God? Or was it a hodgepodge collection of religious documents, all giving "testimony" in some way to what were thought to be "divine events," the central one being that God had taken human form in Jesus of Nazareth? Both "sides" in this volatile debate called the Bible the "Word of God," but they clearly meant two very different things by that same designation. Ironically, numerous social and cultural events, particularly in America, reflected this sharp division over what some called the emergence of "modernism," which became a synonym for "historicism"; the Scopes trial of 1925, for example, had at its core the issues involved in this split over the Bible. Moreover, in the opening decades of the twentieth century this divisiveness over the Bible found its way into the convention halls of virtually every Protestant denomination. In most cases, what had been a single denomination emerged from those convention halls as two denominations, each new one embracing one or the other "definition" of the Bible.[1]

Preaching, too, felt the full impact of this division—but in a strange way. Those on the "conservative" side became the new "defenders of the Bible." Their preaching was given new fodder and fire, since they had a new enemy. They were able to recodify their "fundamentals," and at the top of that list of fundamentals was an unshakable belief in the Bible as the verbal—the word "inerrant" came into use—Word of God. On the other side—called the "modernist" or historical side in the "contest"—a kind of confusion began to surround the pulpit. It was not a confusion about the nature of the Bible, or about the nature or importance of historical critical methods in order to understand the Bible; instead, it was a confusion over how to utilize the "new" historical Bible for preaching. If the Bible itself was a historical book, having natural human origins, then how did one separate out human from "divine" history? If the stories of

the Bible had human histories, if they were created, embellished, passed
down and finally codified in normal human ways, then how did one
distill from the human stories something that might be called a divine
story? If the stories of the Bible were, at their root, stories that arose from
their own social and cultural expressions, then how might our own social
and cultural expressions devise stories equivalent to those "historical" stories? And how, after all, was one to go about preaching, with unwavering
assurance and even some finality, what was essentially a collection of documents from very rich, if very human, roots?[2]

As far as the pulpit was concerned, new thinking about preaching
was clearly needed. It was slow in coming, though, and during the middle
decades of the twentieth century, preaching on this "liberal"—the term
that gradually replaced "modernist"—side of the divide lost its way. Some
preachers managed a kind of dual personality, preaching biblical texts as
the "voice of God" while, at the same time, intellectually embracing the
historical roots and processes of the book. Most, however, now being
trained in historical critical methods in university and seminary, simply
moved away from the Bible itself as far as the pulpit was concerned. The
words of the Bible could no longer be preached with power and certainty
as being God's words. In the pulpit, at least, the Bible gradually was treated
with a kind of benign neglect. Without its "book," preaching lost its edge,
its passion, and the pulpit, primarily in mainstream Protestant churches,
fell into decline. With it, so did the churches themselves.[3]

Preaching, too, fell into decline during the 1950s and 1960s. Books
appeared that asked explicitly, "What's wrong with the churches?" and,
more explicitly, "What is wrong with preaching?" Its power was gone. It
seemed empty.[4] Gradually, a few homileticians began to answer: Preaching has lost its way because it has lost the Bible. What that meant was that
the Bible had ceased within many churches to be the literal Word of God,
or Word from God. The Protestant church, its scholars and preachers, had
turned to "historical critical" modes of thinking which turned the Bible
from God's Word in a direct sense to a humanly created book about religious things. There was nothing left to preach. If the Bible was not God's
explicit Word, a unique book filled with holy words, then there was little—
or so it was thought—to preach from the pulpit. The pulpit had lost the
"biblical preaching" on which it had stood for generations.

Although a number of homiletical books appeared in the 1970s that
tried to "rescue the pulpit," none did it better than one that appeared in
1978, *The Bible in the Pulpit*, by Leander Keck. It was, first and foremost, a
full-blown argument for the recovery of "biblical preaching," but biblical
preaching based in a historical critical orientation to (and definition of)

the Bible.[5] Keck proceeded, then, to devise a view of "biblical preaching" based on this "historicized" view of the Bible. His argument was that preaching is "biblical" not when it uses the text as text to be articulated, but when two things can be said to exist: "When (a) the Bible governs the content of the sermon and when (b) the function of the sermon is analogous to that of the text."[6] There is, Keck contended, a biblical "message" in virtually every text, a "message" arising from past time and place, but one that could be "heard"—a key term for Keck—by using the tools of biblical scholarship.

In short, Keck provided a powerful sense of how preachers who had become, at best, disenchanted with the Bible, unsure of what to do with it in the pulpit—Keck called it a "malaise"—could return to it and actually use it again in their preaching. It was a remarkable contribution to the pulpit, and while other homileticians were saying similar things, none did so with the impact that Keck's book had. The Bible—or at least a historical-critical Bible—would return to the pulpit.[7] What the sharpening of this perspective also did, however, was to crystallize, at least for preaching, the divergence between two radically opposed orientations to the Bible, one that held to a literal text, even if somewhat modified by a weakened Barthian theology, and the other that embraced, without apology, a historical book. The key difference for the latter view, espoused by Keck and others, was that the Christ-event retained its factual and theological uniqueness, while the Bible gave up its literality. The impact on preaching in the early 1980s was dramatic. In homiletics, the new battle that emerged was not over the Bible as such; the new battle was over whose view of "biblical preaching" was to be the correct one; and any survey of the history of homiletical literature from 1980 will reveal two very distinct traditions of "how to" literature for the pulpit—one representing each "definition" of the Bible, and each one contending with various levels of explicitness and passion against the other one.

New Theologies of the Bible Emerge.

By the early 1980s, however, a strange thing began to happen. A series of other theologies, or "definitions," of the Bible began to emerge from the shadows into full view. Ironically, virtually all of these new theologies were a logical outgrowth of the door that Keck and other biblical scholars had so effectively opened, even though neither he nor those other biblical theologians seem to have anticipated the development. At the same time, however, these new theologies arose out of an intensive critique of the historical-critical premises on which Keck's view of the Bible was based. That is, historical-critical methodology assumes a scientific stance, as it were, one based on a scholar's "objectivity" for the discovery of truth, an orientation that, in secular if not in theological circles, was in a shambles as far back as the 1960s. Those behind the new theologies wanted nothing to do with Keck's historical-critical purity, and they weighed in with a major shift in their views of the Bible. We may readily identify three such new orientations toward, or definitions of, the Bible, even though by now each has developed a significant body of literature of its own.

One is the feminist definition of the Bible. Even though the feminist umbrella spreads itself over a number of distinctions, it is possible to identify a common attitude toward the Bible, one that is predominantly confrontational.[8] For feminists, both women and men, the Bible came to be defined as a male, androcentric document, one written by males telling a male history, and utilized by males over the centuries to authorize and assure their superiority over females. By now, the case has been thoroughly documented. In the mid-1980s, a collection of highly influential essays appeared under the title *Feminist Interpretation of the Bible*,[9] that, together, have come to represent a classic statement of the feminist struggle not just to come to terms with the Bible, but to subject the Bible and its texts to a full-blown and unrelenting critique. In essay after essay, from a variety of scholarly and personal perspectives, a feminist theology of the Bible was hammered out and given both concrete and consensual form. The hermeneutic of that struggle became one of reading, interpreting, evaluating, and responding to the Bible from the perspective and context of believing communities of women. It was not just that the Bible contained androcentric language and patriarchal texts; it was more that the whole program of a male savior, the son of a heavenly father, neither reflected nor spoke to the experience of women. One does not, from this perspective, go to the Bible to hear it and speak what one hears, however that "hearing" may be done. Instead, one goes to the Bible because, historically, it stands astride one's tradition, and finding an identity vis-a-vis that tradition requires that the Bible must be coped with. Since the Bible, by and large, is taken to be a barrier to the forward movement of women, an obstacle to the full humanization of women, a feminist theology of the Bible must, in some way, stand in opposition to the Bible, despite its past centrality.[10]

A second important definition of the Bible that emerged in full theological view during the 1980s is the one that has come to be associated with liberation theology. That there is some overlap between liberationism and feminism is easy to demonstrate, and yet there is a significant difference between the two perspectives. Unlike feminism, most liberation theology sees the Bible as the source of Christian faith, as the embodiment of the fundamental story from which Christianity sprang, the story that still energizes and structures that faith. Liberation theology contends, however, that even though the Bible originated as a story of the oppressed, over the centuries it came to be used by powerful classes of people as a means for maintaining their power over the oppressed; the problem, in short, is not so much the Bible itself, but how the Bible has been co-opted and used against the oppressed. The oppressed want the Bible back; they want to find themselves in it again; they want to make it an agent for liberation and empowerment which, liberationists maintain, it was meant to be.[11] But that is not as easy as it appears on the surface, since generations of power and control have built a potent wrapping around the Bible; it is that wrapping that has to be broken away before the Bible can be what it could be. Liberationist scholars and preachers, arising from the grass roots, must bring their full range of experiences and insights to bear on the Bible in order to "break it free." One does not do this for the sake of the Bible, however; it is not the Bible that is primary. The Bible is a potential tool for human liberation; and it is liberation that is primary. It is the experience of oppression that the Bible, once it is freed, must serve. The Bible is, and must be, seen through those experiences. Only then, in fact, will be Bible be understood at all.

Bible as Religious Classic

A third new definition of the Bible has become highly visible and influential since the early 1980s. It has arisen from those who, for want of a better term, we can call the "religionists." These are not outsiders but, by and large, persons who consider themselves Christian, if not by faith at least by tradition. In the past, these were scholars working in religion programs of secular universities and colleges, but increasingly they are part of seminary faculties, working with those preparing for professional ministry. These are scholars (and increasingly preachers) who view the Bible as what David Tracy has called a "religious classic."[12] While that term can mean many things—including many that even Tracy probably does not mean by it—the term itself provides a useful umbrella.

This perspective on the Bible takes up where Keck leaves off with historical-critical thinking. It, too, assumes the historicity of the biblical writings but does not see them as important reflections, or even "recollections," on a historical event or events. Here, the Bible is fully, and explicitly, desacralized, probably more vigorously than even the feminists desacralize it. Those who study the Bible in this way include, and even inculcate, a vast array of intellectual disciplines. Many are part theologian and part historian; many are also part sociologist, part ethnologist, part psychologist, even antiquarian psychologist, part anthropologist, and part folklorist. Often those who work with this orientation to the Bible are interested in it as one "religious classic" in an array of religious classics, the classics, in other words, of the other world religions, both past and present. Often, too, those who work with this orientation to the Bible are most interested in the complex relationships between the emergence of one particular religion, Christianity, and what are seen as its formative documents. These most often are the students of social history, with particular (though not exclusive) interest in social religious history; they are the students of human myth-making, and they see the relatively recent emergence of Christianity as a case study in how humans make, and come to be made by, powerful myths, built around legends of both saying and event.

Many roots of this orientation of the Bible are in the "searches" for the "historical Jesus" in the late nineteenth century; but it has all caught on in a striking new way in the past decade and a half. Best known of these contemporary searches for historical origins have been those carried out by the Westar Institute's so-called Jesus Seminar. Numerous publications are now coming from the seminar, the most widely read one being the group's book *The Five Gospels: The Search for the Authentic Words of Jesus.*[13] The work is unique in that it does function as what one would recognize as a commentary, except that the commentary notes focus on the "probability" of whether Jesus might actually have said the words attributed to him. The work is also unique in that it treats the "fifth gospel"—The Gospel of Thomas, a manuscript discovered in the Nag Hammadi library in 1945, as an authentic gospel, along with the canonical four. For our purposes, what is important is not that relatively few of the words attributed to Jesus in the Gospels are said to have come from his lips; what is important is that such an undertaking itself represents a fairly widespread view among Christian scholars of what the Bible itself represents, what their "definition" of the Bible actually is. The Bible, that is, represents an odd, historically unreliable, collection of bits and pieces attributed to Jesus and those who were said to "follow him"; but there is no biography present in the documents and very little that one could consider even remotely historical. The Bible is a collection of pieces in which early Jesus and Christ communities tried to give voice to their own beliefs, which they codified and tried to disseminate. The Bible is taken to be a secular book, classic in the sense of reflecting the Christ of creed and dogma, but a book, nonetheless, that, because of its admixture of fact and fiction, still pushes every reader to "probe the relation between faith and history."[14]

What is unusual about the Jesus Seminar is that, officially, it believes that the Gospels do, in fact, contain what it calls "historical memories" that might point to specific events in the life of Jesus, something that religionists farther to the left do not accept. In fact, the group's last of what it calls its "seven pillars" makes the interesting point that New Testament scholarship of the past placed the burden of proof on those who argued that the synoptic gospels were *not* historical; as a result, they say, this scholarly work was viewed as negative and destructive. The group points out, then, that its work is based on the opposite assumption; i.e., that even though the biblical narratives are wrapped in both myth and even outright fiction, it is possible to find some kernels of historical data in them as well. So the hunt of modern scholarship—at least of the Jesus Seminar—is not for myth and fiction; on the contrary, it is a hunt for historical germs and gems within the mythology and the fictionalizing. In fact, for many Jesus Seminar members, as well as for numerous other biblical scholars who follow the seminar's work, there is a decided "faith" in the gospel documents behind the work, a faith that does seek to add some historical credibility to the old records.[15]

Not surprisingly, the Jesus Seminar scholars have drawn criticism from what can only be viewed as the left wing of New Testament scholarship. This includes those scholars—and it is a significant number—who simply deny the possibility that anything remotely historical can be found in the remarkable mythic creations that we call the gospels. These scholars fall under the religionist umbrella with the Jesus Seminar participants, but do represent a different orientation to the Bible as well, as the above statement makes clear. One who is prominent here is Burton L. Mack, who until his retirement in 1996 was the John Wesley Professor of New Testament at the Claremont School of Theology in California. Mack, like a number of others who could be cited, is a social historian whose concerns focus on the New Testament and the relationship between its documents and the large questions of human myth-making. Mack has argued that it is simply a waste of time and energy to search behind the New Testament documents for what he calls Christianity's "originating" event, particularly the crucifixion and resurrection of Christ. Such events, he argues, are not merely lost; they have no historical warrant whatsoever. In fact, it is a different question that should be asked, the question that does have power for New Testament studies. That question, according to Mack, is: How did those early communities come to create the complex mythological stories of crucifixion and resurrection, and why did (and do) those religious myths still hold such power over large numbers of people, power that at many points is explicit, but that, at least in American culture, is overwhelmingly implicit? How, in other words, do such religious myths work, and why have Christianity's myths, embodied in the Bible, seemed so thoroughly to capture the Western ethos and mentality?[16]

This view of the Bible, in other words, does not see it as "gospel" in any kind of metaphysical sense; it sees the Bible, instead, as the Christian Church's "charter," its mythic foundational document. It is not historically true, nor was it even designed to be in its various bits and pieces. Its multiple elements were formed at a unique juncture in Western history, at a clear crisis in an ancient religion (Judaism) and the gradual disintegration of several ancient cultures. After explaining the confluence of these profound historical events, Mack notes that the newly emerging idea of the

> kingdom of God called for reimagining society and…it contained both a critical (countercultural) and a constructive (utopian) edge. And we shall see that entertaining such an idea unleashed enormous energy, triggering social experiments that were daring and igniting the most fantastic images of a desired transformation of the world. Social formation and mythmaking must therefore be given a prominent place in our redescription of early Christianity.[17]

That process of social formation and myth-making found its historical expression primarily in the Bible.

Reacting to New Views of the Bible

We shall stop there, however, in order to explore the reaction to the emergence of such dramatic new views of the Bible, simultaneously and in such a short space of time. To do this, we shall return to the work of Leander Keck, who came back into the Bible picture in the early 1990s in a remarkable way, a way that gives us a close-up view of the problem of these various new perspectives on the Bible. After Keck moved from being the Dean of the Yale Divinity School to its Biblical Theology faculty, he was invited to give the Lyman Beecher Lectures at Yale, far and away the most prestigious lectures each year on preaching, lectures that stretch back to the 1870s. In 1993, Keck's lectures were published in a little book under the title *The Church Confident: Christianity Can Repent, But It Must Not Whimper.*[18] While his four lectures were more about the state of North American Protestantism than about preaching, Keck's old concern about "the Bible in the pulpit" had not gone away. What Keck did in those lectures is worth examining in some detail, not only because of the clarity of his statement, but also because his influence remains as potent from this widely read little book as was his book on the Bible, more than fifteen years earlier.

What Keck did as a crucial part of those lectures was to lay out what he called three stances toward or hermeneutics of the Bible, two of which received his hearty approval, while the third he criticized with irony and bitterness. The third is the critical one, one that must catch our eye if we are to understand the depth of the divisiveness that exists over the Bible today. What Keck argued in his lectures was that there is a new hermeneutic afoot in the theological world, one that he labeled a "hermeneutic of alienation." What he identifies as the hermeneutic of alienation is, in fact, at least three hermeneutics, which are not hermeneutics as such, but three views of the Bible—the three perspectives, in fact, that we have now identified as having arisen since the early 1980s. In each case, Keck attacks the new perspective on the Bible, concluding that all of them, taken together, represent a kind of cancer bent on destroying the church from the inside. We need to sketch what Keck says about these three perspectives in some detail, since so many Christian scholars and preachers are working with precisely the assumptions and outlooks that he attacks.

First, it is clear that, for Keck, the feminist orientation to the Bible represents his hermeneutic of alienation. In his lectures, he attacks the growing number of influential feminist theologians, calling their objections to "classic" Christianity "moral objections." He quotes from Patricia Wilson-Kastner's 1983 book *Faith, Feminism and the Christ,* which says that "to refer to 'God' in certain feminist circles is sometimes perceived as a hostile act, or at best one emerging from ignorance." Keck then says that the feminist struggle for a new theology is nothing more or less than a struggle against "the substance of Christianity itself lest affirming it be an immoral act."[19] A few pages later, he mocks another feminist scholar. After stating that "almost any idea gains credence today if its advocates claim to be motivated by identification with the poor, the powerless, and the oppressed," Keck adds: "Even the long-discredited legend that Jesus was the illegitimate offspring of a vulnerable Jewish girl who during her betrothal was seduced or raped, perhaps by a Roman officer (whom the Nazis identified as an Aryan), has been rehabilitated because it is said to show God's concern for the marginalized and the subversion of patriarchy." He cites Jane Schaberg's book *The Illegitimacy of Jesus: A Feminist Theological Interpretation of the Infancy Narratives,*[20] for what can only be taken as a derisive comment.

Significantly, Keck's comments about feminist scholarship, and how feminists do biblical study, are guarded and indirect, though by no means obscure or qualified. The same cannot be said about his attack on how liberation theology views the Bible. His comments about its hermeneutic of alienation are harsh and unrelenting. In fact, Keck has liberation theology in mind when he says that "the motor that drives this hermeneutic of alienation is moral outrage at the world's evils, on the one hand, and the need to deal with a sense of guilt for participating in them and benefiting from them, on the other."[21] Keck's critique of liberationist biblical theology is biting. Christian moral outrage, he says, is not new,

> but it is doubtful whether ever before it has been so potent a factor in theology, for it has persuaded many that the truthfulness of Christian theology must be judged in political terms first of all. Much modern theology has adapted what Karl Marx asserted about philosophy: Up to now philosophers have attempted to understand the world; the task, however, is to change it. No more will religion be accused of being the opium of the people; now it will be the elixir of revolution, for now salvation pertains first of all to the redistribution of earthly goods and power. For centuries the central question of theology, as of all thought, was, Is it true?; in many quarters today, the paramount question is now, Who benefits? That this is a legitimate question is obvious. What is by no means obvious is how it is answered or what span of time is to be considered—though the alienated who have handed out only white and black hats always know.[22]

Keck adds that "with alienation goes the need to identify and to identify with those who are either at the edge or on the bottom of the established system, for such self-identification atones for the guilt of complicity." He takes the argument even further:

> There are only historical—that is, circumstantial—reasons why thus far the theological trend has developed in the name of liberating women, minorities, and the destitute from their plight. But fascism has shown that one can appeal to justice and equity to support also a revolution of the right, because all one must do is to redefine the aggrieved.[23]

Through all of this Keck keeps coming back to his own view of theology and Bible—that the Bible as God's unique "message" of salvation is to be studied "objectively," with a sense of dispassionate detachment, which is what historical critical methodology enables one to do.[24] On the other hand, he says, "the goal of alienation-driven theology is not developing the capacity for independent thinking grounded in a solid grasp of the tradition, but empowerment," a negative statement for Keck, but one with which most liberationist theologians would probably agree. But, Keck adds:

> When the goal is power, whether to hold it or to gain it, the quest for truth is an early casualty. The more theology becomes politicized, the less possible becomes an unprejudiced examination of the issues—precisely what is most needed in our day.[25]

The Scholars of Direct Assault

Keck's third "hermeneutic of alienation" is the one practiced by the Christian "religionists," that growing body of scholars of early Jesus and Christian social/mythic formation; they, too, would reject Keck's characterization of their work as alienating. But this is a particularly dangerous group for Keck, since these are the scholars who have launched a direct assault, even from within the seminaries, against what he calls the "classic liberal Protestant theologies." In the past, he says, these "classic" theologies have confined themselves to addressing such "intellectual difficulties" as the three-story universe, miracles, or a literal Second Coming. Today, though, the new "objections to Christianity," Keck says, do not find particular beliefs objectionable, but find the Christian faith itself objectionable. It is these "new theologians" who represent the biggest problem for the future of the church, as far as Keck is concerned. In their renewed search for some remnants of a historical Jesus, or for the mythological layerings that place such a personage completely out of reach, these scholars have, Keck laments, turned their backs completely on the "classical Christian understanding of the gospel—the Good News that in Christ God has done for us what we could not do for ourselves." What is lost in all of this, for Keck, is classic theology; and he argues, in a sense, that these "new theologians" are in what he calls "wholesale rebellion," though it is not clear what they are rebelling against. What these biblical scholars are doing represents, for Keck, a new phenomenon. "It is not particular beliefs that are objectionable," Keck writes,

> but the faith itself because the culture it shaped is being condemned wholesale. That non-Christians find the Christian faith objectionable is not new, for already the Apostle Paul wrote about the skandalon of the cross. What is new is that the antipathy toward the Christian tradition and its culture now comes from Christian theologians themselves.[26]

Keck adds:

> As a result, the polemical edge of their theology is aimed not at the assumptions and assertions deemed contrary to Christian faith but

against the Christian heritage itself. What was once refuted can now be celebrated as wrongly suppressed truth. Not surprisingly, Gnosticism, polytheism, and syncretism have been affirmed; Manichaeism too has revived, for when this theology is criticized its advocates view themselves as righteous victims in a world controlled by reactionary connivers against righteousness and truth.[27]

Keck's writing about the Bible is unique, since in both his 1978 and 1993 books he gives sharp focus to the formation of at least five different definitions of or orientations to the Bible itself. Some of the differences span a wide chasm, such as the difference between the literal and the historical-critical views of the Bible, and even between the historical-critical view, as represented by Keck himself, and the three more contemporary views. Keck is also important here, however, because, in his two books to which we have referred, he implicitly exemplifies the defensiveness and divisiveness that result when one particular orientation to the Bible becomes what we have described as a hub symbol—held, that is, with enormous emotion, the kind of emotion that turns one's own point of view into a "sacred" viewpoint. Ironically, in Keck's case, in 1978 he was the attacker of the dominant literalistic definition of the Bible, the one that had existed, literally, for centuries. It was Keck who articulated for countless divinity students and preachers a new definition of the Bible, the Bible as a historical book, a book from God to be "affirmed" (as he put it later in his Beecher lectures), but one that was fully conditioned by its historical circumstances; and one that could, with historical-critical tools, be preached accordingly. But that view of the Bible became Keck's hub symbol, and when, over the next decade, other views of the Bible emerged that rejected the assumptions and methods of his deeply held historical-critical view of it, his own "sacred" view of the Bible called for his full, vigorous, and profoundly alienating defense.

The point is that no view of the Bible, no single definition of it, is the correct one, and none is, in itself, sacred. Nor is it feasible to do what Keck does in appealing to Christian tradition for his definition of the Bible, since he clearly acknowledges in *The Bible in the Pulpit* that the historical critical orientation to it, along with its assumptions about the nature and discovery of "truth," is itself a break with Protestant tradition. Moreover, what we call a tradition is nothing more than a definition that has become hardened and extended virtually intact over several generations; at any point, the tradition can be challenged, revised, or a new definitional scheme formulated to take its place, embodying new ways of thinking about and experiencing recurrent situations.

Here, in fact, is the first level of overt pluralism with which the pulpit must come to terms. It is the pluralism of the Bible as Bible, the Bible as symbol, the Bible, more specifically, as hub symbol in the lives of virtually everyone, including biblical scholar and preacher. One can fruitfully begin to preach pluralistically by starting here. The preacher must, as we suggested in a previous chapter, begin with himself or herself. How does the preacher—I, you—define the Bible? This is not to talk about any particular text, doctrine, or theological idea; but it is to reflect on how one defines the Book as Book, and come to terms with that. In this chapter, we have focused on Keck as a way of outlining some—though not all—of the dominant ways of defining the Bible in our time. Beyond that, it requires that the preacher come to terms with the notion that there are numerous other ways of defining the Bible as well, and some of those different definitions will be held by congregants in one's parish. But this said, it is possible to identify some preaching strategies that let one get about the task of preaching pluralistically.

Preaching the Definitions of the Bible

First, the preacher is encouraged to make various views or definitions of the Bible a part of the sermon process. One may, in other words, actually preach that there are numerous ways of defining the Bible, that there are various notions of what "Word of God" in reference to the Bible means, and that there are very different ways by which scholarly people of all stripes go about studying the Bible. For generations, preachers have scolded people for making the Bible only an icon, a coffee-table book to be dusted off when religious people visit; but that, in itself, says virtually nothing, since, to a certain degree, we all do that, religious professionals and laypeople alike. We each have a way in which we iconize the Bible, and whatever study we do of it and however we interpret and preach it grow out of how we iconize it. Far better it would be if, in the pulpit, we could be brought to terms with the multiplicity of definitions of the Bible. This would include discussions of where those definitions came from and how they evolved, what, when and how new definitions emerged, and what the "new" definitions of the Bible are and why they have come into being.

Like all the suggestions I will make here, these are not designed to represent a single sermon on "the Bible," or even a series of sermons. Instead, what I am suggesting is that a deliberate recognition of the multiple orientations of the Bible be a part of one's overall sermon-making;

that it be a part of this sermon and that one, where appropriate, but that one try to create appropriate moments for such material. In my judgment, people in churches (and outside churches) need a sense that there is not one correct view of, or definition of, the Bible. There are multiple views of it, and while each of us will prefer a particular one—even prefer it a lot—it is necessary to keep our own definition of the Bible in the perspective of other definitions, and to help our congregants to do the same. In some ways, this is a crucial form of pluralism that needs to be brought into the pulpit.

Second, it is important, in my judgment, to preach about the large divisions that exist within the Christian world, perpetuated, at least in part, by deeply held divisions over what the Bible is and how it is to be used. Religiously, we live in a largely "us" *vs.* "them" world; and some of the "thems" are fairly close to us, but some of the "thems" are as far from us as possible. In many communities, ministerial associations show the results of these divisions over the nature of the Bible. Often, there are at least two such associations in the same small town, one made up of mainstream Protestant ministers, often with some Catholic priests or other leaders, and the other fundamentalist ministerial group, held together by their common view of the Bible as the inerrant Word of God. But the Protestant world is more fractured than that, even; and virtually everywhere one looks, regardless of the social roots of this body or that one, the divisions tend to be identified and perpetuated by a particular definition of the Bible. To preach pluralistically is to make the nature of these divisions a part of one's preaching. It requires discussing the Bible and the Bible's often basic role in such divisions. But it will also be preaching that calls people to an inclusive attitude toward those who live and work on the other religious banks.

Finally, one should be encouraged to preach about the social, cultural and personal roots of one's own definition of the Bible. The preacher can readily incorporate his or her own struggle over the Bible itself, of growing up with a particular symbol of the Bible and then tracking how that view was shaken, or changed, or thrown out, or recast, or whatever. This is not a single statement that one should set out to make, but, as suggested a moment ago, it should become part of the motif of various sermons that struggle with the Bible. The preacher, in this context, may deal with the ways in which our views of the Bible become hub symbols, making us defensive, creating hostilities toward those who, we discover, have different views of the Bible. What one is looking for in such exploration over time is a sense that one's hub symbol of Bible is not, for any given person, a "God-given" view; that is, that our various definitions of the Bible, however emotionally we hold them, have come to us from someplace in our past. We do not hold them because they are "from God" and no other views can possibly have any legitimacy—even though, honestly, that is the most common sense of an individual's view of the Bible, since that is the nature of any hub symbol. One need only remember Professor Keck's view of his historical-critical definition of the Bible to see that the hub symbol process works for biblical people of all kinds.

All of this, in my view, should be set in an ongoing context of teaching the Bible as Bible; that is, as canon and extra-canon. One is encouraged to spend less time with texts themselves and more time with the history of the Bible and the Bible's early communities. One should preach about historical-critical process and what it has taught us over the last couple of hundred years. It is not that such preaching is particularly devotional or inspirational, but it is very important for our contemporary processes of thinking, and living, and knowing how to be religious. One should preach from, and about, feminist perspectives of the Bible; one should bring the feminist critiques and understandings of the Bible into the pulpit—explicitly as well as implicitly. One should, whatever one's congregation, bring to light and life the liberationist understanding of the Bible, as well as the various concepts related to the Bible. One should also be part of preaching about the insights of the Jesus Seminar scholars and of other scholarship related to Christian myth-making, both past and present. These are profoundly important things, even though we are not used to thinking about preaching in such terms. These, though, are ideas that shape our minds and our attitudes toward the church and, more importantly, often toward each other, both within a particular Christian community and across the boundaries that so sharply separate our Christian communities. At the heart of it all is the Bible itself, about which we must, somehow, preach. There is a gospel of pluralism, and it is a pluralism of the "book."

5

Pluralism and the Text:
Kenneth Burke and the Art of
Symbolic Exegesis

Preachers preach biblical texts, whether directly or indirectly, whether to affirm them or to confront them. No matter how one approaches the text, the process assumes that one can decipher the meaning or meanings of those texts. Yet, as every preacher knows, that is considerably more problematic than it sounds. The fact is that exegesis, or the uncovering of biblical meaning, is one of the most tangled and confusing dimensions in all of Christian theology. Theories of exegesis or hermeneutics are every-where, usually complex and esoteric, most often requiring skills and re-sources that confine their use to experts and scholars. From Romantic and Idealist theories to semantic, structural, semiotic, discourse, and nar-rative theories, the hermeneutical landscape tends to leave even the most conscientious preacher in a paralyzing fog. As a result, the preacher's week-by-week exegesis and interpretation of a text is often done by the seat of the pants.

The exegetical questions are not easy ones. Does a biblical text have only one meaning, or does it have multiple meanings? Is it possible that its meanings are unlimited? How do texts come to be written? Can one ever know what an author of a text meant when words were put on paper (or on whatever)? If so, how? Or if not, why not? How are we to preach the meaning of a text, if we cannot ever be sure what it is? Does, or can, a text mean anything one wants it to mean? If so, doesn't that destroy the whole idea of meaning itself? These are important questions that lie at the heart of biblical exegesis, questions from which the preacher can never escape.

Text—any text, including biblical text—is also a pluralist phenomenon; most hermeneutical scholars now share that view. Explaining how
or why it is, and how that impacts our understanding of text, though, is
not something that is done well these days. Those who originally worked
out the premises and concepts of symbolic interactionism did not themselves devise a textual, or hermeneutical, theory, so it may seem beyond
the scope of this study to consider its implications for the handling of
text, particularly biblical text. That is not the case, however. Their orientation to text is implicit in their focus on symbols, and "words as symbols,"
as well as in their own early studies of the written documents of a culture.[1] But what was implicit quickly became explicit when Kenneth Burke,
a young literary critic, entered the picture in the early 1930s. He began to
produce what came to be a full-blown symbolic theory of text, based on
interactionist assumptions and principles. So, even though we have utilized some of Burke's observations throughout this study so far, we now
turn to Burke for a full-scale orientation to text based on the symbolic
principles that we have found in Mead and the symbolic interactionists.[2]
When we turn to Burke as our guide through symbols and text, moreover, we also turn to one who Wayne Booth, the literary critic, has called
"one of the great pluralist minds of our time"[3]—a statement that is in full
harmony with this study.

Burke's roots in the 1920s and 1930s were in literary criticism, and to
a lesser extent political theory, but not in sociology or social psychology.
Early on, however, he was reading and absorbing the ideas of Mead and
the social psychologists at the University of Chicago. Even though he was
largely self-taught—which was always one of his problems in the world
of academia—by the time he published *Counter-Statement* in 1931, it was
already clear that his view of the symbol and symbolic action would embrace the unique and even revolutionary perspective of the symbolic
interactionists. This perspective, for Burke, was summed up in an explicit
repudiation of what he came to call the "semantic" view of language, that
is, a view of language as neutral and attitude-free. It meant, instead, that
he embraced and began to explore what he called the "poetic" view of
language, meaning language as emotion-charged, as laden with an implicit attitude.[4] The word "attitude," in Burke's use, means a particular
orientation toward whatever the term or word indicated, with "emotion"
referring to intensity, either negative or positive, toward that term or word.
Since language, like all symbols, is emotion-charged, it is used not just to
express those emotions, but also as a means of using those emotions to act
in the world in highly charged ways.

Semantic vs. Poetic Ideal

For Burke, what he called the "semantic ideal" was substantially different from the "poetic ideal." The semantic view of language, he contended, attempted to "get a description of something" by the elimination of any attitude toward it—something that Burke held not only to be downright impossible but even destructive of language. The poetic ideal, on the other hand, sets out to get a description of something precisely by coming to terms with all of the conflicting attitudes toward "it" and piling those attitudes atop each other. Semantics would try to abstract, if not eliminate, all emotional factors from the terminology that would complicate its "objective" clarity of meaning. The poetic view, Burke's view, would derive its terminological vision precisely by grasping the emotional factors involved in the language, "playing them off against one another, inviting them to reinforce and contradict each other, and seeking to make this active participation itself a major ingredient of the vision."[5]

This starting point is important since so much contemporary hermeneutical theory, particularly among theologians and biblical scholars, has adhered rigorously to what Burke has called the semantic "ideal." It is this, however, which ties Burke so intimately to the symbolic interactionist framework. It also means, though, that whereas many literary scholars create two classes of language—the language of the poet or writer and the language of "common usage"—Burke sees only one kind of language used for common speech as well as for poetic bursts, in effect, from it. This is important because it enables Burke to see text, of whatever kind, as an extension of human "conversation." In other words, what happens when humans interact in a face-to-face encounter is not unlike what happens when humans encounter the "voice" of another in textual form. Again, this viewpoint stands in contrast to much contemporary hermeneutical thought, which wants a qualitative break between human conversation and reading a text.[6]

What takes place, in short, in a human-text encounter is essentially the same thing that takes place in a human–human encounter; and this, in fact, is what makes possible the paradox of how and why a text, any text, can have multiple meanings and yet a single meaning. For example, in a conversation involving several people who take their turns speaking and listening, when one person speaks and the others listen, each one listening places his or her own meanings on what the speaker is saying. This is, in fact, the fundamental premise of the symbolic approach to language and behavior that we have developed from the beginning of this study. Each listener, moreover, reacts to what the speaker is saying, not in terms of the speaker but in terms of the meanings and emotions that the particular hearer has brought to the conversation. If, for example, the speaker is talking about the joys of having had a happy upbringing, but one person in the group did not have a happy upbringing, then the speaker's words are, in a sense, rejected or at least "responded to," whether overtly or not, through a filter of negative symbols. Other hearers would have different responses to what the speaker is saying—some, no doubt, drawn to him/her by shared positive symbols, others by still different symbols. The same thing is true, Burke argues, with textual materials that one reads. One reads words and paragraphs on a particular subject—the writer is trying to "say" something, as in a conversation—and one "responds" to the words through the filter of one's own symbol system, particularly one's own "hub symbol" system.

This is the basis, in part, for the view—now common, though not well understood—that a text not only can have, but has, multiple meanings. A text, in fact, can have a vast number of meanings, limited only by the number of people who read it. Each person will bring his or her own symbol system to the text and through that unique symbol system will give that text its meaning. This is, moreover, the basis for the idea of what has come to be called contextual meaning, referring to the fact that different communities, with their own symbol systems, give their own meanings to a text—in our case, to a biblical text. Thus, the African-American "reading" of a text will be different than a Korean "reading" of the same text, and so on as the contexts become smaller and smaller, reaching down to each individual's unique reading of that single text.[7]

This, though, is only the beginning of the paradox of meaning. There is another dimension to it, this one also drawn by Burke from the model of the conversation. This one suggests that, even though every individual participating in the ongoing conversation brings his or her own symbolic perspective to the conversation, when one speaks to others, the one speaking always has "something to say," has something in mind that he or she wants to say to the others. By the same token, Burke argues, when one writes a text, whether an essay, a biography or a poem, the writer has something particular and deliberate in mind, and that act of writing becomes one side of the human interaction of "reading." The words are there, on the page; they are objectively present. Someone selected them, devised them, arranged them and had some particular effect in mind during all of those processes. The words on the page are loaded, i.e., charged with emotion and viewpoint, just as all symbols are.[8] They have all the properties of all symbols, whether they are spoken, written, acted or otherwise fashioned and shared.[9] Moreover, the act of creation results from an impulse or the prolonged germination of something that one wants to say, often passionately so. Behind the words is an idea, something that someone wants to communicate, however articulately or inarticulately it may actually come into being. Burke has probed deeply into the ramifications of why and how one writes, not only creating complex meanings, but beginning with the germ of an idea, a notion or an attitude, and then constructing forms that will give maximum force to what one has in mind.

The Text as a Perspective

Every text represents a specific, and often unique, perspective, set up on its own terms, created to give form and voice to that perspective. This is the second dimension of a "pluralist" text. From Burke's point of view, since a text exists on its "own terms," in its own terms, it must be dealt with in those terms, whatever they are, however they are intended to act in the world. In Booth's words,

> Instead of thinking that we can refute a given position by showing that it cannot be experimentally or logically falsified, we are *invited by it to one perspective on the world*, a perspective that is likely, by the very nature of perspectives, to be self-demonstrating. Every perspective expressed in a symbolic language becomes a "terministic screen" which both reveals some truths—obviously "demonstrated" to anyone employing the language—and conceals others[10] [my emphasis].

The question, then, is not whether a particular text is distorted or not, because something is distorted only in relation to a different perspective. There is no standard of meaning or truth apart from the ways in which various cultures and individuals themselves set a particular standard, and then what will be a distorted viewpoint from an outside perspective can become the norm or standard from within that perspective itself. What Burke and symbolic interactionists are interested in is the nature of the similarities and differences that maintain between and among the endless number of perspectives that cultures and their creators devise and sustain in textual form. Again, to quote Booth's comments about Burke:

> He in fact rejects more than conventional norms. His dialectic of similarities and differences is so deliberately flexible and so aggressively opposed to neatly fixed meanings that in a sense all literal proof is made suspect.[11]

At the heart of this orientation, however, is the question of whether one can ever understand what a particular writer meant or even had in mind in the composition of a text. Many contemporary scholars like Paul Ricoeur contend that one cannot; for him, the issue of "what a writer meant" is moot. As Ricoeur put it at one point, "We have to guess the meaning of the text because the author's intention is beyond our reach."[12] While one must, of course, acknowledge the difficulty of understanding an author's meaning, or intention, it is not, from Burke's point of view, that we have to guess the meaning of a written document, any more than we have to guess the meaning of someone who is speaking to us face-to-face. Do we always know the meaning of what one says in conversation? Of course not. But there are many ways of developing one's listening and empathic sensibilities that in dialogue give one access to what someone else's "outlook" is. Ricoeur would reply that, in a face-to-face encounter, "validation" is possible in the ongoing conversation, since one can keep asking, "What do you mean?" and the other can keep answering—which is not possible in written communication. Burke would in turn respond that no matter how often one asks in face-to-face encounter, it is still words, i.e., symbols, that are exchanged, and that one set of symbols does not necessarily "validate" another set of symbols; they simply become part of an ever-growing string of symbols. In fact, Burke probably would argue that in face-to-face conversation the symbol strings are fleeting and can sometimes be lost in the very process of speaking; on the other hand, with a written document the words themselves are at least "fixed"; they lie still on the page so that one may actually look closely and even analytically at them. For Burke, the chances of grasping their meaning, or the author's intention behind them, is much greater in written than in conversational speech. In fact, a significant amount of Burke's work over the years has focused on literary methodology, on devising ways to get a sense of a document's own "point of view." If a text represents one perspective (as a speaker represents one perspective), as Burke contends, then one should be able to probe far enough into the words to somehow come to terms with that perspective.

Burke's Textual Assumptions

How to do this, then, is the question Burke asks. His textual methodology, rooted in symbolic interactionist theory, is unique, or as Booth would say, unconventional. It is based on three fundamental assumptions. The first should be obvious by now; it is that, for Burke, a text of any kind is always a part of a larger ongoing situation (i.e., "conversation") out of which it emerged, and to which it makes its own unique contribution. This is one of the major differences between Burke and what came to be called New Criticism, which assumed that a text existed as a unique document that could be fully understood in isolation from virtually everything. Burke, in fact, begins the long title essay of *The Philosophy of Literary Form* by arguing that all writing of a critical or imaginative type represents an answer to questions, or a question, posed by the situation out of which it arose. Moreover, the text is not merely an "answer"; it is a "strategic" answer, or a "stylized" answer, since, as he put it, there is a difference in both style and strategy if one says "yes" to imply "thank God," or to imply "alas." Burke contends, moreover, that this view of text in no way commits one to either personal or historical subjectivism. As he says, the situations are real; the textual strategies for handling them arise from the public domain; and "insofar as situations overlap from individual to individual or from one historical period to another, the strategies possess universal relevance."[13]

Thus a text, Burke contends, can and must be deliberately and systematically studied on its own terms, as we shall see shortly, but it is never written in a vacuum, nor can it ever be fully comprehended apart from the situation for which it is a verbal (i.e., symbolic) strategy. This means that one who would understand a text must attempt to discover all that is possible about the larger historical and sociological circumstances out of which the text emerged. The ongoing conversation of that larger arena is necessary to grasp the unique contribution that any particular text makes to the historical conversation. Granted, this is never done perfectly, particularly when a work is produced in a drastically different situation than one's own. This does not prevent, however, the deliberate and fruitful study of the text itself, since it, in fact, usually contains multiple clues as to the conversation in which it takes its place. So Burke moves to the study of text itself with that understanding in the background.

The second assumption is that one must always let a text "speak for itself." Burke devises what will be recognized as a kind of "structuralism," but he argues that most structuralist theories, like positivist literary theory, set up their "categories" of meaning before they even begin to work. What Burke wants, instead, is as pure an "inductive" process for the analysis, or exegesis, of text as possible. His contention is that, even though a writer must work with the words or terms of one's own language and grammar, everyone who writes places his or her own meanings, both cognitive and emotional, into the symbols and words that one selects; it is the symbolic premise on which the symbolic tradition is based. Thus, the critic or reader cannot—as positivist language perspectives do—assume that one knows in advance what words or forms mean when they are used in a text. Nor can one assume that one can say in advance how the grammatical and syntactic structurings of a text's form will figure into the creation of meanings or emotional weightings. Writers write in order to change or even construct new meanings, new images and linkages, new symbolic configurations having emotional twists and turns most writers hope will not be readily predictable. So one who reads is asked to set one's own meanings aside and try to grasp what a writer means by this term or that one.

Burke does not contend at any point that his analysis makes one's reading of a text automatically free from subjective judgments or inter-pretations. What he does contend, however, is that his procedure forces one to set aside any absolute meanings with which one comes to the text. One cannot, that is, say what any term in the text means before one begins work on that text. One only learns the meanings of the text's language by an "inductive inspection" of the overall work itself. Then one discovers, as it were, the particular contexts, and even unique meanings, that the writer devises for this part of the work or that one. It is the writer's overall "equational structure" that will provide the text's mean-ings, as well as the ways in which those meanings may be changed by the writing in the course of the text's unfolding itself.[14]

Burke's third important assumption is that in both speaking and writ-ing two levels are always at work.[15] A text, that is, has a "surface" dimen-sion; it is an above-water string of words, grammatically or ungrammatically laid in tandem, the lineup which one actually "reads." However, under-neath that surface is a vast network of collected and created ideas, of symbolic meanings and patterns, all shot through with attitudes, feelings, emotions, perspectives, values, etc.—all of those dimensions that we said constitute and represent one's hub symbol system. This is the hidden part of the meaning system, the iceberg under the water. For Burke, every writer writes from the resources of that vast hidden domain within one-self; and what one writes on paper represents one's turning that hidden, symbolic world into a narrow stream of visible substance. And while the surface words may, on their own, convey linear meaning—the text "says this" or it "says that"—one must always wonder and search for the larger, formative meanings that are under that linguistic surface. A writer may, in fact, use the surface stream of words to belie what is underneath; one may try, that is, to use the words to "get by with something," to be untrue as far as the hidden meaning or meanings are concerned. This is commonplace, in one sense; and yet its implications for an understanding of text are often overlooked.

The Text as Conversation

This means, in short, that what one encounters in a text is not sub-stantially different from what one encounters in conversation. We are used to calling it "saying one thing and meaning another," and we are prone to think that we can tell it by the tone of one's voice or the look on one's face during a conversation. But we are also aware that often such is not the case. People can and do hide things under their language, as it were, structuring what they say in an effort to control how others will respond to them. We know well about irony, that process of saying one thing, but by the very form of the words meaning something else. And while Burke says that one must take full account of such elements in speech, this is not what he has in mind in this premise. What he means is that a writer (or speaker) has a sense of what he or she wishes to convey, an attitude toward something that he or she wishes to embody in words. To do that, the writer usually draws, in an unintended or unplanned way, on his or her internal reservoir of symbolic attitudes and materials. This means that language clusters and forms of expression come to the surface of the page, some of which, in retrospect, may even surprise the writer who laid them out. It is a deeply important aspect of textual creation for Burke, one that cannot be described better than Burke himself does:

> [One] organizes an essay. He necessarily chooses certain pivotal ver-
> balizations about which he hinges his discussion. He chooses these
> particular verbalizations because they *appeal* to him. Some other terms
> might be substituted in their place, so far as the pure logic of the case
> is concerned. But he makes a selection in accordance with the subtle,
> personal tests of "propriety." Though the words are, on their surface,
> neutral, they fit together into an organic interdependent whole pre-
> cisely because of their common stake in some unifying attitude of his.
> We may get cues prompting us to discern the underlying emotional
> connotations of words that even the user may consider merely "sci-
> entific" or "neutral." By locating these, we get glimpses of a subtler
> organization than is apparent when we take the words at face value.[16]

While the surface of the text, as it were, is "littered" with words, it is not a random littering; but neither are its patterns immediately visible and deducible.[17] As Burke puts it, the writer's

> selectivity [with language] is like the selectivity of a man with a tic.
> He squints or jerks when some words are spoken, otherwise not.
> You disclose the "symbolic organization" of his tic when you have
> found the class of words that provokes it. Similarly, the [writer's]
> selectivity is tic-like—and the discovery of its organization is per se
> the discovery of its symbolic aspect.[18]

Meaning can be said to lay within the words of the text; but to assume that what is on the surface of those words is the full bore of a writer's meaning is to fall victim to a writer's easy tricks and subterfuges. For

Burke, the meaning to be deciphered is in the underlying, usually hidden, "symbolic organization" beneath the words and how they are strung together on the page. The surface words, then, must always be read against the backdrop of the crucial underlying text or textual layers.

How, though, does one uncover this submerged meaning of a text? One does so, Burke argues, by inductively dissecting the text's symbolic organization. At the heart of Burke's literary output is a methodology, something that separates Burke from virtually every other prominent literary critic of the twentieth century. The methodology is spelled out carefully in a few places, illustrated profusely in others, and commented on, in one way of another, on page upon page of his writing. His methodology is ingenious and relatively easy to use, which means that it is readily available to preachers and their biblical texts; moreover, it is virtually always fruitful. The remarkable thing about Burke's literary methodology, which he usually refers to as "analytical exegesis," is that it is a straightforward process of inductive textual "deconstruction"—though Burke never used such a word—which he devised long before Jacques Derrida fashioned and made popular the notion of deconstruction. Burke believed that for meaning to be found, the surface of the text had to be upset. It had to be spaded up, burrowed under, penetrated, and broken apart in order for one to discover its undergrowth. One did not break down the text for the sake of breaking it down, but because the intentions or the motivations behind the text could only be uncovered by overturning the text's surface.

Burke devised a simple set of procedures for doing that—and for doing it inductively. Burke proposed what he called the "theory of the index," the basis for his literary exegesis. The process is one that does nothing more, in its initial stage, than to turn the horizontal text into a vertical one. Unlike a normal index of authors or topics, such as one finds in the back of a book, this index is a listing of the text's words in vertical order—but, as Burke puts it, in the order "of their appearance" in the text itself. The words are not alphabetized, but are listed in their chronological order. This is the remarkably simple deconstructive process, as it was developed by Burke. By thus breaking down the horizontal, or reading, formation of the text, this process forces the eye to destroy the text as it is normally read. This disorienting turn of the text from a horizontal to a vertical form allows for a fresh, or naive, working through of the text; it makes possible a fresh tracking of the text's terminology and underlying symbolic formation without being confronted by a preordained, prior, or linear meaning. From a visual point of view, this index-making permits the eye to look at each term "as a term" before moving on to terminological relationships. As a result, one's consciousness of the words themselves is enhanced. This means, first, that each term can be accounted for "in itself" as well as later within its concordant setting. The second thing about the index is that it can be as comprehensive as one wants it to be. While Burke says that the index should contain all of the text's "key terms," he is quick to point out that one cannot know in advance what terms will be key ones; so one devises an index which contains virtually all of the nouns, verbs, adjectives and adverbs in the text, as well as most prepositions and all transitional terms, whatever they are. In cases where the text is relatively short, every term in the text may be included in the index. We will illustrate the making of an index by taking a recent lectionary text, the text from which we will devise a sermon in the Appendix of this book. Here is an "index" for Luke 24: 44–53:

Then	should	power
he	suffer	from
said	third	on
These	day	high
are	rise	Then
my	dead	he
words	repentance	led
I	forgiveness	them
spoke	(of) sins	out
to	should	as far as
you	preached	Bethany
while	in	lifting
I	his	up
was	name	his
still	to	hands
with	all	he
you	nations	blessed
Everything	beginning	them
written	Jerusalem	he
about	you	parted
me	are	from
in (the)	witnesses	them
law	(of) these	was
Moses	things	carried
prophets	Behold	up

must	I	into
be	send	heaven
fulfilled	promise	And they
He	(of) my	returned
opened	Father	Jerusalem
their	upon	with
minds (to)	you	great
understand	But	joy
Scriptures	stay	continually
He	in the	in the
said	city	temple
(to) them	until	blessing
Thus	you	God
written	clothed	
Christ	with	

One will note that some articles and particles are omitted, but care should be taken in leaving out even the most insignificant word. It is impossible, as we suggested a moment ago, to know in advance what word—even a single word—may turn out to be important to the writer. Once the index is constructed, then the text itself is set aside so that the index can be the focus of concentration. What, then, does one do with this index? While Burke has given some rather specific instructions for handling it, there is no foolproof procedure that one can learn. What happens next is a kind of detective work, and different eyes will see different things, with each making a case for this particular discovery or that one. There is data here, though—the words on the page, strung together in this specific order; and so one must always be willing to return to the data in making judgments about what the text is "made of," about what it might mean. The problem, though, in saying what a text like this means is that it may often have one meaning on its face, in its surface construction or assertions, and a very different kind of meaning—a motivational or ideological meaning—in its deeper symbolic layers. And this procedure of the index is designed to reveal those deeper meanings as a counterpoint, in a sense, to the surface statements. We shall see in this text what we might find.

Burke's most systematic discussion of a methodology of text—his "theory of the index"—is found in a 1954 essay, "Fact, Inference and Proof in the Analysis of Literary Symbolism." There, he proposes some directions, or guidelines, for working on the index; he wants to know, he says, how to "operate with these 'facts' (i.e., words), how to use them as a means for keeping one's inferences under control, yet how to go beyond them, for purposes of inference, when seeking to characterize the motives and 'salient traits' of the work, in its nature as a total symbolic structure."[19] Once the index is created, one literally stops "reading" the text and starts studying it as a list or arrangement of particular and carefully selected terms. One now works with the index in what Burke lays out as the second step of the exegetical process. It is the construction of what he refers to as a "concordance." A concordance is a clustering of terms together by any kind of relational principle—a principle not so much of the critic's making, but of the writer's making. One goes looking, in other words, for any terms that seem to be "alike," terms that are, in any way, related to each other as terms. Again, this is all done inductively from the index list without any prior sense of what the relationship of similitude might be. The assumption is that, whether deliberately or not, the writer will cluster words throughout the text that belong together in some way within the writer's mind. The terms that cluster together, wherever they are found in the text, may be words for colors, for references to earth elements, terms for happiness or gloom, terms that are distinctly religious in character, terms that suggest family relationships; and so on. Every text, by its nature, will probably reveal three, four, a half dozen or more different sets or clusters of such terms. These clusters make up the concordance of a particular text, a concordance for analytical purposes only and not to be seen as any end in itself. To construct a concordance, one simply starts looking, thumbing, hunting, listing, doodling, comparing, reflecting.

Let me take you back to the text from Luke 24 for which we made the index a moment ago. After going down the list from top to bottom a few times, I started by picking the word "words," connecting it to words for speaking or writing or something like that. I thought they would go on for a while, but they did not seem to. I ended up with "say" and "speak" words—words that together were "communication" terms. Here was the list:

said	said
words	preached
spoke	witnesses (I will put it here, but not sure)
written	blessed? (will put it here, but not sure)
Scriptures	blessed—at very end

These are terms that emphasize the communication process involved in the text, but what is significant as I comb the list looking for them is that they only appear in the first half of the text. If one drops out "witnesses" and "blessed" at mid-text, they end halfway through—except, of course, for the word "blessing," which does seem to imply speech, at the very end of the text. I will set the list aside for now and go on. I am struck by what I will call the religious language of the text; others may want to call these terms by some other designation. My list becomes quite long:

law	Jerusalem
Moses	Father
prophets	heaven
psalms	blessed (here is where it probably belongs)
Scriptures	Jerusalem (again)
Christ	blessed
repentance	God
forgiveness	

We would expect this, of course, since this is a "religious" text, a text about "our religion," so it is our religious language. So we take note of it. These are religious people. They are a combination, in a sense, of Jewish (since Jewish language is present) and Christian (since Christ language also is here). It is an interesting combination of such words. But I will set it aside for now, too. Now after going down the list a number of times, I am struck by one particular set of unusual terms, unusual language. It is what in my doodling I now label as the "up" language. The list is not long, but it is striking by its repetition; and it only appears toward the end of the text. Here is what I have written down:

from on high
lifting up
carried up

For Burke, language in a text can take on significance in two ways. The first is by the frequency of its appearance; frequency indicates importance, emphasis. The second, though, is by the intensity of a particular term or set of terms. Intensity is usually indicated by unusual terminology and by its placement—at beginnings or endings, or at points of denouement or climax. The "up" language, in this case, seems to be important on both counts: by its unusual "up-ness" and by its clear clustering at the end of the text—not just this text, but the entire Lukan text.

Still, after making these concordant clusters, I kept going down the index, feeling that I was missing something, that there was some kind of terminological pattern here that I was having trouble finding. It was only after I laid the text aside for a while and came back to it that I saw something that, to me, became very important, something that was so obvious I kept overlooking it. I began to make a new list:

he	I
my	my
you	you
my	you
I	he
you	them
I	his
you	he
me	them
he	he
their	them
he	they
them	
his	
you	

The list startled me at first, I think, with its run of personal pronouns. My first question was whether or not this would be normal for a narrative piece of writing. So I checked at random some story pieces, not related to biblical material. I concluded that it is fair to say that this proliferation of *I's, you's, them's,* and *they's* is unusual and very significant. Its significance is found in the fact that the Gospel of Luke is not an eyewitness account, particularly not this "story" at the end of the Gospel. It is a mythic story, devised by someone in a particular Christian community two or more generations after Jesus walked in Palestine. This is a story of a community devising its own history, its own apology for its particular faith. The pronouns, whether they are I, you, or they, are the words with which these people refer, in a real sense, to themselves, as well as to those who give them their history and identity. The pronouns are all ways of talking indirectly, about themselves. This is a self-possessed community, insisting on its own special—indeed, its own exalted—place in the world. This is an ego-building text for the community, a text that represents a case study in self-definition of a very particular kind, or so it seems to me.

Now we are talking about the motives, the intentions, underneath this text; and in my judgment we have worked our way to its bedrock. If we now play these intentions off against the surface meanings of the text, the emphasis of the text becomes poignant. For example: *We* are the ones, the text is contending, who know the secrets of the ancient writings. We are the true interpreters of the writings of Moses and the prophets and even the psalms. We are the ones who have seen those scriptures in their entirety "fulfilled." We are the only ones—and this is a key phrase in such an intense assertion—who have had our "minds opened" to "understand the Scriptures." We are the ones whose lives are now "blessed" in such a way that "we" can call others to repentance and can mete out forgiveness. We are the only ones who are now "sent" to "all nations." We are the chosen "witnesses." We are the ones that Jesus, the Ultimate of God, chose to bless. We are the ones who received the crowning promise from God. We are the ones who have been "clothed with power from on high." We are the ones who were commissioned as Jesus left for heaven. We are the ones who, with great joy, bless God. The pronouns lay down the track of the text, and the other clusters give form to those pronouns. We are a religious community, one created by the words and the voice of God, a community "from above."

Following Burke's methodological directions, this is my "reading" of this text. Others may read it in different ways, may do their exegesis of it quite differently. This is what, for me, an inductive searching of the language and its construction yields; and my task, at this point, would be to think about how one says in a sermon what one finds in the interaction between the text's surface "story" and its underlying assertions and emphases. Can one develop a positive, constructive sermon, having done this kind of exegesis? I think so; and in the Appendix I will devise a sermon based on this exegetical analysis.

Inductive Exegesis as Practical Process

It is the uniquely inductive nature of this process that still sets Burke's textual methodology apart from the multitude of "criticisms" that dominate both secular and biblical literary hermeneutics. It is also the uniquely simple nature of this exegetical process that makes it so usable by preachers on a week-to-week basis in the handling of biblical texts. What the work invariably produces, when the preacher takes the time and care to do it, is a substantive and often strikingly original orientation to virtually every text to which it is applied. One is used to preaching the "story" of the text, whether narrative, parable, or miracle, or the didaction of the text, whether of aphorism or epistle or doctrine. What Burke's analytical exegesis produces is a radically different body of "information" about the text, a sense of its undercurrents, its assumptions, implicit ideas, unspoken definitions, and veiled assertions. How, though, will all of this figure in effective preaching, particularly preaching that seeks to be pluralist in its outlook? In at least three ways preaching can be deeply and significantly affected by this form of exegetical work.

First, this approach to a text, to any biblical text, regardless of genre, provides a way for one to preach in full, overt interaction with the text itself. This will not be just referencing the text, providing some notes from one's study about the text. It will, instead, involve the preacher in a serious conversation with the text, a conversation that can and should often be shared as part of the sermon. One will query the text, letting the text, as it were, "have its say" within the sermon itself. It will not involve the preacher in reiterating or reviewing the surface narrative or didaction of the text, as important as that might be. But congregants very often have heard all of that before, know what is coming, and must somehow summon up the energy to hear it one more time. What Burke's methodology of the text makes possible is a new and deeper insight into the text's own "outlook," not as a verbal phenomenon, but as a sense of what—as far as we can conjure it up—constitutes the underlying concerns and perspectives of whoever produced the text. One presses behind and under the text, taking it apart and pushing it, as in a face-to-face conversation, to "explain" what it is getting at. One asks the text to "talk about" its own structure and form, about its own perspective, about why it says what it does about whatever it is talking about. The text picks the subject, and the preacher's task—at least as far as "preaching the text" is concerned—is to press behind the surface subject for the text's own motivation and underlying symbolic organization.

If this sounds irreverent as an attitude toward the biblical text, it is not. It does, as we suggested earlier, involve one in what has come to be called a deconstruction of text. One must read the text carefully and open-mindedly, noting its grammar and its assertions. Some of these elements, of course, may find their way into the sermon, or may even form some basis for what will be preached. But the text, if we are to come to terms with it, both in the study and in the sermon, must be *taken apart*, turned over, deconstructed, in order to see behind and under it. What, in other words, motivated the text?—and, for Burke and symbolic interactionism, those motivations are hidden in the symbolic clusters that one must deliberately and systematically "tease" from the text's deep structure. Thinking congregations, however, want in on all this. If they are interested in biblical text—and they are in significant numbers—they will want to share the preacher's probing of the text; they will want to be in on the conversation with the text's deepest motives and hidden agendas. And Burke's methodology, applied to biblical text, provides information for that encounter with text that is both simple enough and interesting enough to make a part of the sermon itself.

A second way in which Burke's symbolic exegesis can affect preaching is in the way it allows texts to be set in tandem with each other. Sets of lectionary texts are designed to be used together, though it is a rare preacher who can actually do more than take one of the two or three recommended texts and comment on them thematically, theologically, or in some other way. There is reason to wonder why certain texts are placed together for lectionary purposes, but usually it is because of a common term or common theme or theological tone. The methodology that Burke provides enables the preacher to apply the same systematic procedures to various texts that must "stand together," as it were; and it enables the preacher to study not only the surface dimensions of multiple texts but the underlying symbolic systems of those texts. While it may be that on the surface some common ingredient has attracted attention, under the surface the texts may stand at opposite ends of the hallway; under the surface, the concerns or motives of the several texts may reflect vastly different outlooks—or even similarities of outlook that no one has suspected.

It is not uncommon for biblical theologians to call attention to the fact that the Bible, in all its diversity, reflects countless perspectives, both individual and collective; in this sense, the Bible is often described as a thoroughly pluralist document. Even the New Testament, they will point out, does not have a single, unified viewpoint or theology. Matthew's theology is not Luke's; the Synoptic outlook is not that of John's Gospel; nor is it easy even to argue for a consistent theological viewpoint as one moves from one of Paul's letters to another. This so-called pluralism of the Bible is needed in the pulpit. The problem has been that preachers, by and large, have lacked a workable, inductive, methodological tool for honoring and exposing those differences of viewpoint or theology, however subtle they may be. Burke's orientation to textual analysis provides such a working process, one that may be applied to different texts on the same subject in order to reveal the underlying concerns or motivations from text to text. Again, these are matters that, if handled with care and sensitivity, can and should find their way directly into sermons. The desire to "look more deeply into the scriptures" ought to be more than a cliché. Here is a way in which it can be more than that—and sermons that reflect such study will be gladly heard by thinking congregations.

There is still another way in which Burke's methodology of text can contribute to the sermon, one that, in the final analysis, may be the most important of all. It is that Burke's orientation provides a way for the preacher—and the congregation—to confront and challenge a text, to expose what is often called these days a text's "ideology," its undergirding thought pattern. It is a way, systematically, to say, "Here is what this text says on its face, its surface, but when we dig under the text here are some of its 'other motives.'" And one can say such a thing without guessing, without undue speculation, and without finding this or that under a text simply because one "wants" to find it there. What one looks for, though, is "evidence"—what Ricoeur called "validation"—of what can be demonstrated from a systematic deconstruction of the text's symbolic structure. One can ask the text to demonstrate its ideology, its underlying notions and hidden concerns; one can ask this of a biblical text. If this sounds somewhat devious, it is not. It is a part of coming to terms with the nature of what text is and how it works; and biblical texts are no more or less devious than any other texts. This is a way, however, that the preacher can, with honesty and integrity, analyze and evaluate a text, and, shall we say, reject it—not "out of hand," but "for cause." Burke's methodology gives one a means for determining what that "for cause" might actually be.

Here is a way for us to cut through the beauty of well-known texts to see what they are made of, to discern what their underlying messages, symbolically clustered and framed, actually are. Here is a way for us to *ask* our questions of the text, and not let the text control all of the questions and the answers, as our surface studies of text can sometimes tend to do. We can ask the text to talk about gender issues, issues of pressing ethical importance, about pluralism and the integrity of other religions; and we can, inductively, press under the glib answers and evasions of the text itself to uncover what the text's authors might really have had in mind. Virtually every text has its own surprises. The biblical texts are profoundly ideological, in some ways more ideological than theological. The ideologies of text—and the roots of those ideologies in ancient cultures and religions—need to be coaxed to the surface so they can be examined for what they are. Here is a methodology that works to expose those ideologies, whether they are personal, political, or cultural. Here is a process for studying text—and preaching the results of one's study of text—in a way that can bring new interest in the Bible to the pulpit; that exposes biblical text, not only to find something good in it, but also, with integrity, to turn text away.

Burke's approach to text should be known by preachers; it is usable, productive, and provocative. What it produces need not just undergird the sermon or the sermon's orientation to a text; it should find its way *into* the sermon. It should do so, however, not with any measure of certainty, as "this is it"; but it should do so in a probing way; as a way of asking questions about the text, a way of coaxing the text, a way of *not* taking the text at face value, of not letting the text off the hook with what it seems to say. When one preaches this way—and helps thinking people press in this way under and around a text—one's preaching takes on a sparkle that, instead of demeaning the Bible, will actually give the Bible a vitality that it can receive in no other way.

6

Pluralism and the Gospel: Prophetic Otherness for the Postmodern Pulpit

It is clear that there is no longer any unanimity about what the Bible is; the Bible is a pluralistic document. Nor is there any unanimity of response to any particular biblical text; what we hear in a text and what we say to a text can vary with every perspective and individual. So when we come to the most fundamental question of all, why should we expect the situation to be any different? If we ask What is the gospel? we are forced to respond that there is no single answer, not even a generic one, that will satisfy everyone. Different theological systems conceive of the gospel in very different ways, as we should now expect that they would; and appealing to the Bible or even to a set of specific biblical texts is no longer of any help.

The problem, however, is that for centuries, Christian faith, theology and preaching have been based, even from their roots in Judaism, on an absolute sense of the "gospel." That gospel has been built around the correctness and certainty of a set of interpretations about the figure of Jesus—about his identity, his vocation on earth, his extraordinary powers, and his singular role as the resurrected God of human history. What we are now confronted with is that the absoluteness of such theological assertions, whatever they be, has been a mirage. What we have believed, particularly about Jesus, we can continue to believe as a way to give spiritual meaning and substance to the lives we live. We can even take our beliefs as ultimate for our own lives, as we choose to do. But it is no longer tenable for us to assert our beliefs about Jesus—about divinity, about resurrection, about his being the only path to God—as final, complete, and unalterable for every human being everywhere. This is a deeply disturbing notion, to say the least, particularly for preachers, whose very livelihoods have depended upon those precise affirmations.

At first glance, it would appear that such a conclusion would mean an end to Christian preaching, since to preach is to preach the gospel. Such a conclusion, however, is simply not justified. What it means, instead, is that the idea of gospel itself must be rethought and reformulated. We not only can still preach—we *must* still preach. But we must take full account of emerging new realities of life, theology, and the intricacies of human struggle. We want our preaching to count. We want our sermons to be vibrant and affirming—but affirming of what? Of gospel, yes—but what is that? Or, rather, what is that in a pluralistic world in which the very idea of gospel has either been splintered into a thousand pieces or has become meaningless altogether? It is not so much that our sermons must "preach the gospel"; it is now that our sermons have to be part of discovering gospel—not necessarily "the" gospel, but "gospel." And, when we come right down to it, we still want our sermons, even in these pluralist times, not only to be uplifting and challenging, but even prophetic. But can they be? The answer—if we look deeply into where we have been in this study—is Yes, they can; but grasping that, and putting it into practice in our pulpits, will revolve around thinking in a new way about the idea of gospel and of what we might call our "theology of gospel."

The symbolic interactionist tradition on which this study has been based is not about theology per se, even though the motivations of its early pioneers arose explicitly from issues that surrounded the social gospel. However, symbolic interactionism probes into the very heart of the materials out of which all theologies are constructed—symbol, language, definition, self-consciousness, and human interaction, to name only a few. As a result, it not only can say something about the nature of theology, and theology's gospel, but it has an obligation to make itself heard. This, though, is jarring at best for both theologians and preachers. Theologians, for the most part, would prefer that theology give its evaluation, its critique of symbolic interactionism, and even pluralism. The problem with that, however, is that contemporary pluralism is more to be described than critiqued; and the power of symbolic interactionism is in its ability to describe what has happened—and why—in the contemporary world. One of the things, in fact, that comes under that descriptive umbrella of symbolic interactionism is the nature of religious and theological symbolization, or perception. In short, the relevance of symbolic interactionism for the church is that it provides a powerful social-psychological critique of Christian theology, or, rather, theologies, including the myriad formulations of the Christian gospel. One might also hope that it would be something of an obligation for theologians—both theoretical and practical—to attend to what this perspective might say about the gospel.

In retrospect, symbolic interactionism would assert the need for theology and Christian preaching to take full account of three overriding axioms—an axiom of "relativity," an axiom of "universality" and an axiom of "otherness." The three are intricately related, and when they are taken seriously, they lay the groundwork for what could well be not only a new understanding of the Christian gospel, but a renewed sense of what the purpose of preaching might be in the coming decades. Each of these must be taken up here as a basis for devising what we might call a pluralist gospel for a reinvigorated, perhaps even a prophetic, pulpit.

The Axiom of Relativity

The first is the axiom of relativity. The single most obvious, and difficult, implication of symbolic interactionist theory is that meaning of any kind—including religious meaning and Christian theological meaning—is a human, i.e., a symbolic, construction. There is a world of objects, to be sure a world of "things." There are elephants and accidents and things that go bump in the night. Whether there is a similar invisible world, a spirit world or whatever, no one can say for sure. And the idea of these things as "real" can certainly be insisted on. What matters though—and this is the point of symbolic interactionist theory—is that nothing takes on reality in the human mind and experience until it is given meaning by the human mind; until, that is, it becomes a symbol by being given meaning and emotional weight. Every human being must do this; and every human being does it differently, even when two persons point to what appears to be the same thing. This means, as we have seen from the beginning of this study, that all symbols are relative, which is another way of saying that no two symbols ever mean exactly the same thing for any two people. Every individual—even when we can talk about the shared symbols of a given culture or group—brings his or her own subtle and complex meanings to that symbol. The whole premise of this perspective, in fact, is that meaning does not arise from fixed or transcendent symbols, nor does it ever inhere in symbols, regardless of what they are. As a result, all human meaning, tied as it must be to symbolization, is unique and virtually always creative. Symbols—*symbols*—are never fixed, nor are they ever absolute or universal. They are limited to cultures and collectives that create, use, and maintain them, however widespread such use might be.

Does a symbol mean what anyone says that it means? The answer is yes, for all practical purposes, since for each individual who uses that symbol, it does. Writing—and preaching—are ways of explicitly giving one's own definitions to symbols, definitions that one hopes that others will, if not adopt, at least consider carefully and appreciatively. This is not to say that we do not learn common symbols of the groups in which we are nurtured—we have seen clearly that we do—but even as we are learning those symbols and assimilating the meanings that our groups give to those symbols, we are combining them in unique and often spontaneous ways, and we are placing our own created meanings into them as well—something that we all do throughout our lives.

All of this is true for religious symbols and symbol systems, of which the gospel, however it is construed, is one. No two meanings of God are ever alike, despite (fortunately) considerable overlap within groups who share the same understanding of God. No two meanings of Bible are alike, as we have seen. Nor do any two individuals, even in the same groups, define any element of worship or liturgy alike. One Christian's idea of gospel is not another Christian's definition of gospel. When one crosses the widest religious boundaries, from religion to religion, one can say that "we call God this and you call God that, but we are talking about the same God"—such statements are easy and to some extent, no doubt, valid; yet there is no way to minimize the relative nature of religious experience. And, at bottom, the problem is that no one—absolutely no one—is in a position to say whether one person's idea of God, or worship, or Bible, or even gospel is "God-given," while others' are not.

Facing this, however, is what brings us to the problem for Christianity, and for Christian preaching. It is that Christianity must come to terms with its own relativity. This is not a value statement; it is an axiomatic statement. Christian beliefs, like all beliefs, are symbolic constructs, valuable symbolic constructs; but symbolically devised, just as all religious beliefs are devised. Entirely apart from what kind of God or gods may actually be said to exist, our understandings of God, our senses of how God acts toward us and through us, our beliefs—including our hub symbol beliefs—about what God has done "for us" or will do for us are all dimensions that we conceive and maintain symbolically, in language, image, ritual, and theological argument. As we said at the outset of this study, it is immeasurably difficult for us to actually grasp the full import of our symbolic natures, which this asks us to do. There are no symbolic absolutes; they not only do not exist, they cannot exist. There is no unchanging norm for what the gospel is; as we have seen, we live in an age in which any theological norms left over from the past have been completely overturned as new theological thinking takes shape.

Does God exist for all time and place as "one God"? One can affirm, "on faith," that that is an absolute statement, and yet we are affirming a symbolic belief statement, and the evidence of history, sociology, and religious study is that all we can say is that most people seem to symbolize some kind of ultimate force, which they, in turn, call by many different things. The same is even truer when we speak about our Christian "belief" that Jesus is "God's Son" and, as such, the "savior" of all humankind. Such a statement clearly absolutizes something that is symbolically limited, confined, that is, to a single religion, while other religions have their own "saving" or "purifying" dimensions and rituals.

The Relativity of the Past

This is, by no means, the first time in recent years that Christian scholars have tried to find ways of dealing openly with the problem of religious relativity. In the 1960s a few Christian theologians began to come to terms with the relativity of religion, including Christianity. Not coincidentally, it was about the same time that the "rediscovery" of symbolic interaction theory was taking place. The theological effort, however, quickly became caught on a barb that, in its popularization, obscured the issues that it was trying to raise; that barb was the "death of God" language. What became the death of God theology was a seminal argument that Christianity, because of its historicity, was as relative a religion as was any other great religion. As John Cobb put it at the time, "We cannot but understand ourselves and our beliefs historically and hence relativistically."[1] The Christian religion arose within history, within a particular set of cultural circumstances, as epochal as they were, and its ways of envisioning God and God's manifestations on earth were shaped by that unique historical milieu. By implication, as that milieu shifted or even vanished, replaced by new circumstances, the understandings of God that arose "back then" would have to shift and change as well. So a particular way of "thinking about" God—a particular way of defining God—died as it were; and new ways of thinking about God were not only called for, but indispensable. By and large, however, that message did not come through the death of God movement; it was dismissed as quirky and quacky.

In the mid-1980s, another group of Christian scholars gathered at the Claremont Graduate School in southern California not just to discuss religious relativity and pluralism, but to confront the issues, and each other, as directly as possible. What emerged from that series of meetings was an important collection of essays, which by the mid-1990s had already gone through five printings. It was titled *The Myth of Christian Uniqueness: Toward a Pluralistic Theology of Religions*. What the book demonstrates is that at the heart of the problem of religious pluralism is—still—the power of the absolute, the Christian absolute, since Christianity, from its inception, has contended unequivocally for its uniqueness among all religions, for its one-and-only ("only begotten") status. It is this unrelenting argument for uniqueness which, "in much Christian discourse...has come to signify the unique definitiveness, absoluteness, normativeness, superiority of Christianity in comparison with the other religions of the world."[2] It is this uniqueness that the book's editors designate as the myth that must be overcome in a pluralistic age. The dividing line, in fact, that seems most clearly to separate what has been called the modern world of the recent past from the postmodern one of the present is that the modern world still believes in absolutes while the postmodern one contends that absolutes are dead, if they ever actually existed.

Ironically, the "prophetic" model that has come to Christian preaching from the Hebrew prophets is one based on "certainty" and an unshakable belief that what one has heard is the clear and pure "word of God" to be delivered to people reluctant to hear it. What is different here is not that the need for prophetic preaching has passed; instead, what is different is that prophetic preaching in a pluralist vein becomes a call to uncertainty, to a sense of human and religious limitedness. It is an affirmation that what we think we know certainly and absolutely is, in fact, neither certain nor absolute. What we know and believe is neither final nor exclusive; our minds are limited, the range of our symbol systems is finite, and the way we symbolize things—even our religious faith—is as circumscribed by our situations and definitional processes as is that of any other human beings, who hold faiths and beliefs radically different from ours. That, in short, is what we might call the new prophetic preaching, and it is as difficult for many Christians today as were the messages of the ancient Hebrew prophets for those ancient people of God.

One may then turn this "affirmation" around to see what might be called the "evil" that it addresses—the evil, as it were, that takes limited symbols and symbolic beliefs, even Christian ones, and turns them into ultimates, absolutes. It is taking the finite and giving it infinite status. Kenneth Burke argues that there is something in the nature of the human symbolizing animal that is always, innately, pressing to do this. For Burke, it is in the nature of human action, i.e., the symbolizing nature, itself, something which, as he says, makes the human species "rotten with perfection."[3] Humans always want to turn their own limited symbols into ultimate symbols, insisting that they should be "everyone's symbols" as well. What is "good for me should be good for everybody"; what saves me should, by its nature, be what saves everyone else. To accept limitedness, in fact, and to grant authenticity to the symbol systems of others, however different those symbols may be, is an extraordinarily difficult thing to do. Yet—or "so"—to preach the limitedness, or finiteness, of one's own symbols, or ideology, or even one's religion, even Christianity, becomes a pressing message, a prophetic and courageous message, for a pluralist world. For the pulpit, this is the crucial "so what" of this first axiom. The finiteness of our own religion, of our Christianity, needs to be preached as a major, creative theme of the pluralist pulpit. *It is not a negative, but a positive theme.* It is an affirmation about who we are, set in the context of where we have come from; more importantly, though, it is an affirmation of who others are whose religious ways are different from ours. Neither our ideology nor our religion are normative for others. It is time for us to examine ourselves in light of others. It is time for us to probe into our own perceptions of ourselves, our own theologies, and to do so, with restraint and courage, from the pulpit. It is time prophetically to call ourselves and our church to the finiteness that our pluralist world requires of us.

The Axiom of Universality

There is a second axiom that arises from symbolic interactionism, and it is the axiom of "universalism." At first this does not appear to follow what we have just said; and yet, in reflecting on the tenets of symbolic interactionist theory, one grasps what this means. Usually, to affirm relativity, as we have just done, is to conclude that nothing is fixed, that there are no foundations whatsoever on which one can stand, that, as they say, "anything goes." And yet absolutism and relativity are not the only two options, as far as symbolic interactionist thinking is concerned. There is a third option, a kind of middle ground. What scholars like George Herbert Mead have contended from the beginning of this century—and what Kenneth Burke brought to fullest expression—is that all humans share a set of "universal" traits, or, better, abilities.[4]

Mead considered them innate abilities, and we have already taken note of what they are. While these abilities may, in some cases, be tied to the functioning of human senses, often these abilities transcend even sensory restrictions. The first and most basic one he called the symbol-using ability, the instinctive ability to "pick up" symbols—i.e., language, etc.—without being expressly taught to do so. The second innate, or universal, human trait, for Mead, is the "empathic" ability; that is, the instinctive human ability to take on the meanings and feelings of another person by utilizing that person's symbols. For Mead, this is the basis for what he was the first to call "role-playing," or getting inside of someone else's symbols. The third innate human ability for Mead is the "reflexive" ability, by which he meant the ability of every human being to become an object to himself or herself; that is, the ability to react to oneself in the same way that one reacts to someone else; this is the trait that makes human society-building possible. With these traits, Mead argued, humans work together in various kinds of arrangements to create and sustain cultures, as well as shared ideologies, religions, forms of entertainment, and livelihood.[5]

Within the broad tradition of symbolic interaction that emerged through the century, no one else developed the sense of universals beyond Mead more than Burke. In the early 1930s, Burke published a book entitled *Counter-Statement* in which he picked up the notion of human universals, beginning with the "root" of human symbolicity, or the innate capacity to use symbols. Later, Burke would write his well-known essay titled "Definition of Man" and place the symbol-using ability as the first of his "human traits." In *Counter-Statement*, though, Burke went beyond the innate symbol-using ability to discuss a series of other elements that he contended are also universal to all human life and experience—he called them the "constants of humanity."[6]

He identified four sets of these "constants." The first set he called the "innate forms of the mind," among which are the sense of "crescendo," "contrast," "comparison," "balance," "reversal," and so forth. The second set Burke labeled the "recurrent emotions," including experiences of such things as "fear," "tenderness" and "delight." All symbol-using humans, he contended, seem to share these kinds of "emotions" in common, regardless of culture, time, or place. The third set he called the "fundamental attitudes," including such things as "belief," "cynicism," "skepticism," "expansiveness," and "reclusion." For Burke, any survey of human cultures, past or present, will show the presence of these "attitudes," even though how they are actually embodied or expressed varies widely from culture to culture. The fourth set of "universals" Burke identifies as "typical" or "universal experiences." Among these are experiences of "despair," "wonder," "lamentation," "hatred," "hopefulness," and "relief." For Burke, these are universal "because all (people), under certain conditions, and when not in mental or physical collapse, are capable of experiencing them. Nor does it matter whether we choose to call them mental or somatic; it is sufficient that they arise," and they arise virtually always out of the relationship between the human "organism" and its environment, most notably other people.[7]

The idea is not to become embroiled in Mead's or Burke's categories, or how others have said similar things; it is, instead, to understand that, underlying the relativity of cultural, mythic, and religious symbol systems is a common set of human symbol-using abilities. There are no absolute *symbols*, no universal codes of conduct, ethics, or religion that are always and forever true. Nor are there any items of absolute truth, immutable and unchanging, any more than there are any transcendent conceptual structures that are fixed for all people at all times. This does not mean, however, that there is nothing but pure, unadulterated relativity; it does not mean that we can know nothing or believe nothing, since nothing, ever, is sure. It is not that kind of either-or situation. The argument, in fact, is that these universal symbolic traits or abilities bind humankind together, as unfailingly diverse as our symbolic forms of life, culture, and religion may be. We have no absolutes of religion or theology—they do not exist—and yet we do have what we might call an "anthropological universal" in our common human symbol-using capacities, as well as in our seemingly endless capacities for spinning highly creative symbolic processes, structures, and systems. We of the human species are intimately related to one another, across both time and space. We are part of one another. We are connected. We can experience our interrelatedness. We are creatures whose minds and psyches work alike, and though we may express ourselves in endlessly different ways, in culture, ideology, and religion, we are connected, regardless of how we look, how we talk, how we worship, how we face both life and death. We are not adrift. We do have a sense of foundation, even though we must ultimately find it in ourselves, in both our human connectedness and our human finitude.

Again, too, there is what we can call, for want to a better term, an "evil" side of this dimension, something to which preaching must give constant attention. It is the rampant denial of human commonality, a rejection of essential human oneness. It is the deliberate and destructive creation and fostering of barriers between peoples who are different in whatever way. This is where all of the "isms" of culture, race, ideology and religion come into play. Often the creation and maintenance of human barriers are so deep as to become almost invisible. But racism is the maintenance, even advocacy, of fundamental "difference" between races, a process, however subtle, by which one race "affirms" its superiority over other races. There is the demonic "classism," by which one economic or social class asserts its superiority over other classes. Lines are drawn, chasms are created, differences in "kind" are touted. This axiom that arises from symbolic interactionism embraces the fundamental sameness, or oneness, of all humans, asserting that this oneness is in our common creation, our common human qualities and abilities of symbolicity. It is our common image, however it originated. This is more than just a philosophical argument, more even than a theological tenet; it is also, at its most basic level, a psychological and sociological affirmation, a "finding out" about who and what we humans actually are. It is this that can be affirmed in preaching. In many places and circles, it is not popular preaching; it is, however, as truly important and prophetic in our day as were the prophetic utterances of the Hebrew prophets in theirs.

The Axiom of Otherness

There is a third axiom, one which is, in a sense, based on the first two; it, too, arises from symbolic interactionist thought as one of its clearest and most influential strains. It is the axiom of "otherness." We began this study by pointing out that symbolic interactionism emerged as a theory of human conflict, born at a time of enormous social and political turmoil. Its earliest scholars were focused on the problem of how and why humans did not get along, why communities, once tenuously formed, broke apart so easily, and how and why human conflict, in all of its manifestations, seemed to dominate the modern world. Needless to say, those are still the issues that maintain a hold on us. Our problem, still, is how to accept each other, how to share with each other, how to grant to each other a certain autonomy of idea and religion, and, ultimately, how to disagree and resolve differences with dignity, with an acceptance of diversity, and even with a sense of hard-nosed, non-authoritarian compromise—and not with cruelty, aggression, hatred, bloodshed, and even massacre.

From its very beginning, the symbolic interactionist tradition saw the answer to the problem of human conflict in the seminal concept of the "other"; specifically, in the process of how one came to "define the other." Paraphrasing W. I. Thomas' fundamental dictum, "How one defines the 'other' shapes how one acts toward that other." By implication, to *change* how one acts toward a particular other or "set" of others, one has to change how one actually defines that, or those, others. More than any intellectual tradition of the twentieth century, symbolic interaction has explored the concept of the other and the complex phenomenon of otherness. George Herbert Mead worked through the idea of how others around whom one matures shape one's self-image and outlook—an idea that many scholars in recent years claim to have discovered. Mead also coined the idea of the "generalized other," that social definition of a particular "other" that comes to be shared throughout a culture; again, a concept still much used but with little understanding of its origin or original intention. Harry Stack Sullivan, the great psychologist, drawing on Mead and the symbolic interactionists, devised the concept of the "significant other," a term that in popular contemporary usage has become an inane designation, but one that originally was a highly original and creative concept; it referred to those "others" who one comes to define in highly positive ways and who thereby are consciously assimilated into one's own outlook. In recent years, new scholars in the symbolic interactionist tradition have made a concern with the "other" a key part of their research; they have tried to take seriously Thomas' dictum that how one defines the other in a particular situation shapes how one acts toward that other in that situation.

The idea of "otherness" is a corollary to the idea of "universality." What we have called human relatedness connects us intrinsically with every other member of the human species—it makes us, in a sense, family—and yet otherness points up our separateness from one another at the same time. It highlights our differences, something that our symbolic natures make possible. We are one as a species, and yet we are not. And that is the source of our conflict, our intense rivalries, of what appears to be the warring nature of the species, potentially over anything, including religion. The question thus comes down to the matter of how we symbolically define all of the others who are part of who and what we are. And how we define each other in our myriad situations shapes how we treat each other.

Ironically, there has been some rediscovery in recent theological circles of the notion of the "other" and "otherness"; in fact, it has emerged as something of a characteristic concern for postmodern speculations. For example, the Jewish philosopher Emmanuel Levinas has made "otherness" and "other-directedness" the centerpiece of his thought. In a sense, he has returned to the work of another Jewish scholar, Martin Buber, whose classic, but sketchy, I-It, I-Thou categories of the 1920s echoed the concerns of the symbolic interactionists, whose work he undoubtedly knew. The other, as Buber expressed it, is not to be an "it," which connotes both detachment and depersonalization, but a "thou," which expresses, on the other hand, the dignity of human personhood for the other. While Buber sought to express the value of dialogue in his distinction, Levinas in his recent work has gone further, arguing that one has a unilateral obligation for the "other."[8] In contemporary postmodern ethical theory, the other has emerged as a crucial concept; one can see this demonstrated, for example, in the work of Zygmunt Bauman.[9] For the most part, though, these scholars have not gone much beyond a keen awareness of that other, or an emphasis on the fact that we are not alone, that we a part of "others" and that they are a part of us. What is still missing—and what symbolic interactionism can contribute to a reframing of our understanding of gospel—is a sense of the dynamic intricacies of otherness in our lives. The fact of the other is not the issue, as important as that is. It is not an acknowledgment of the presence of the other; it is not even a sense that "we are them and they are us," though those are indispensable insights. What is crucial, instead, is how we actually *define* the "others" who live and move and have their being around us everywhere, who make up the multiple worlds in which we live.[10]

How, in other words, are we to identify and define the wide range of others, whether we encounter them face to face, as collective others, known to us through filters of ethnicity, culture, gender, or even religion; or whether we encounter them through institutions—i.e., I know you because you belong to such and such a group? Our problems with each other are wrapped up in our difficulties in defining each other. Our prejudices, our hatreds, our stereotypes are all definitions of "other" people. Our manipulations and violations of other people, of each other, are virtually all based on specific, though often buried, definitions that we make of each other. Who is my neighbor, and how am I supposed to act toward that neighbor? Who is my brother, and how shall I treat him? Who is my sister, and how am I to behave toward her? Who is the stranger, and how many different kinds of strangers are there—and how should I react to, and interact with, those myriad strangers? Who are the "others" for whom I work, who are, as it were, above me, who have power over me; and how am I supposed to define and act toward them? Who are those under me, over whom I have significant control, whether they are employees, students or children; and how am I to define them in my daily dealings with them? Such questions take us to the very core of biblical story and image. Such questions form the heart of theological reflections, wherever they are found in the pages of the Bible. Even as you have done it to the "least of these" you have done it unto me, Jesus reportedly said. By how you love and treat (define) one another shall those around you know that you are "my disciples"—this principle became a foundation of the earliest Western theology. We are trying to give new form and drive to those sentiments.

Who Are My Neighbors?

Such questions of "human definition" are at the center of the complex, even perplexing, human lives that all of us live. They are the questions, seldom articulated but lived out hour upon hour, by those who come to our churches. Why are my neighbors the way they are? How am I to define those who act out hatred and violence up and down my street? How am I to make sense of the kids and teen-agers who frighten me when I go out of doors? How am I to respond to the terrors, big and little, that people inflict on each other with random anger and violence? The world is out of control, and we are both puzzled and terrified by it. What are we to do? What are the answers? The questions proliferate, and they are the pressing issues of contemporary urban life. Here is the place where our sermons become probing and touching, the place where our preaching reaches directly into the lives of people. How, then, shall we live?—which means, How, then, shall we define all of the others who surround us, in person and in image, in the course of a given day?

Preaching can work in the theological nether lands, of course, as it has for a long time; but the result will continue to be what we have watched so gloomily over the past several decades: people will simply forsake the church; it will have lost its appeal. People need help, definitional help; and they will go where they find it, whether that help is good or bad, which, to some extent, accounts for why so many still turn to fundamentalist, charismatic churches and preachers—no timidity there for offering ways to define the human dimensions of the world. However, the definitions one tends to find there are destructive, divisive definitions, not pluralistic ones. But for mainstream Protestant churches and preachers to recapture the hearts and minds of contemporary people, we must enter the down-and-dirty fray of addressing—if only to question and explore—the problems involved in defining and acting in the daily world.

It is not just a matter of how to deal with "strangers," not just xenophobia, as important as that is; the fact is that some of the difficult definitional problems we all face are ones involving people we know very well. It is a matter, though, of focusing, one by one, with insight and sensitivity, on the vast multitude of very different others who surround us in our pluralistic patterns of living. It is a matter of breaking apart the biblical cliché of "love" and translating it into proposals for attitude and stance and empathy, as best one can. It is a matter of humanizing those who are, or have been, dehumanized, of thinking aloud about traps of human stereotype, prejudice, and self-superiority that become the behavioral bases for the grossest forms of injustice and violence. It is a matter of re-defining "others" in real, human terms, not to excuse inexcusable behaviors, but to develop a sense of both human commonality and difference.

For example, think briefly about who some of these "others" are, with all of their differences, and the potential problems that surround how one defines them, problems that have no ready or easy answers—ever.

First, there is what we might call the Familial Other, whether parent, child, spouse or ex-spouse, whether in-law or stepchild or foster child, whether grandparent, grandchild, or live-in companion. Law enforcement officials tell us that some of the worst possible relationships, the source of some of our society's most cruel violence, are the relationships of family. We know about spousal abuse and child abuse, how pervasive they are. We know about abuse of the elderly, particularly when they are kept at home. We know about stepchildren and multiple household children of second and third marriage parents. We know about the emotional fires that can simmer for long days and nights and suddenly erupt. What many preachers know very well, too, is that a startling amount of familial abuse and violence takes place among those who on Sundays are church people. How, though, should the parents define their children? How should the family define the elderly person living in their house? An enormous difference is made if one defines that elderly person, however subtly, as a "used up" individual, essentially good for very little, or if one defines that elderly one as a "wise and interesting" participant in the span of the twentieth century. Different behaviors rise and fall on those different definitions and others that one could propose. How should a husband define his wife and the wife define her husband? It becomes clear that certain definitions almost call for abusive behavior toward the wife and that if that definition could somehow change, the behavior itself might undergo change. Can one find preaching places here? Can one see the variety of ways that sermons could be formed around the process of helping people define and redefine the Familial Other?

There is also the profoundly important Racial or Ethnic Other. Wherever one turns today, there are racial animosities and divisions and often they are intensified by the closeness with which people of different colors and ethnic origins now live and work. Strides have been made in breaking down the old so-called "color barriers," at least in some aspects of life, and yet racism still seems to infect everything, even the church. We can talk about the need to "see no color" or nationality, but until we begin to think seriously about how we actually do "define each other," or define those who are ethnically or racially not like we are, we will not begin to press toward some sense of social and cultural change. It is both personal and societal, both interactive and cultural. Do we define each other across racial lines in human, mutual terms of commonality or relatedness; or does some kind of subhuman definition come creeping in, however subtly, in language or innuendo? Do we define those of other ethnic origins, whether Asian, American Indian, African American, Spanish or Mexican, or whatever, as reflecting "God's image," or does some kind of demeaning image shape our definition? Our treatment of those who are "not like us" rests, ultimately, on how we define them. Even this process of definition, though, can become more complex than it appears to be on the surface. For example, one can have a friend who is of another race or ethnicity, someone who is close and even admired—the two "know each other"— and the definition of the other in that friendship is of the highest order; and yet that individual definition does not necessarily carry over into the definition of all those of that particular ethnicity. We can find ourselves defining the individual and the collective differently.

There is what we might call the Economic Other, the one who, through wealth or poverty, lives in a different world than does the "middle class." Usually we do not see or know these people territorially or "in person." We know them, though, as we know the majority of people in the world, in image or stereotype; we know them generically, as it were. Yet we define them collectively—both the wealthy and the poverty-stricken, including those who live on various kinds of welfare—and our collective definition of them shapes our behavior toward them in a multitude of ways. If we define those on welfare, whatever the nature of their poverty, as somehow lazy or inferior, then our behavior toward them collectively, and even toward any single person we might see and identify with, will be shaped accordingly. On the other hand, if we define them in some other way, as trapped or "cut off from the social family" or however, then our behavior toward them, and those we see and identify with them, will be dramatically different. The same thing is true, ironically, when we define the immensely wealthy in our society. If we define them as evil in some way or as greedy or whatever, our behavior in their direction will be shaped accordingly; and so forth.

There is also the Religious Other, a deeply important one for pluralist preaching. How does one define the other of a denomination that is not one's own? Since, for many, it is in the context of one's own church that one is "saved," is the other saved by his or her church as well? What about across the Protestant/Roman Catholic lines? What does religious tolerance mean when one talks about the "religious other"? Then one begins to consider the others of other religions—those who are Jewish, Muslim, Buddhist, or whatever. By and large, American church people do not know how to define these others, do not know how to even think about them; and this is clearly an area where help from the pulpit is deeply important. In years past, when one lived largely within a Protestant community, such matters were of little urgency; but no more. Now, these are pressing issues, and help in definition of the religious other is simply not available—if not from the pulpit.

The list of identifiable Others can go on and on. The New Testament is filled with comments about those large numbers of people who are other by virtue of being oppressed, disenfranchised, or discriminated against, the outcasts of societies or even communities. These exist in every country around the world, even in the United States, and as majorities in most poverty-stricken countries. In numerous countries, they are women, still shrouded under male definitions that must somehow be broken. They exist also as children, countless children, even in the most developed countries of the world, including the United States.

Toward a New Theology of Preaching

For many, the question at this point will be how theology fits into all this—if, in fact, it does. It does, we should say, but it will not be the old theologies which have an absolutism or a sacred kind of fixedness at their core. At least two contemporary theological streams, only tangentially related, may be said to feed into the approach to preaching outlined in this chapter.

First, some will recognize the affinity between this orientation and the so-called "process theologies." It is not coincidental that a philosophical process theology owes its existence to John Cobb, the theologian commended at the outset of this study for his courageous acknowledgment of the pervasiveness of relativity in religion, indeed in Christianity. Cobb drew on Alfred North Whitehead to devise a theology that saw even the idea of God in emergent, rather than in fixed, terms. More than that, though, process theology takes a giant step away from the host of traditional, or orthodox, theologies that are fundamentally "transcendent" in character and language. Whether process theologians acknowledge it or not, they have created a theological motif which not only translated theological language into anthropological language, but which actually locates the presence and meaning of God in the human sphere. They have laid out the parameters for an "immanent" theology. In days gone by, theologians liked to talk about God as dialectically both transcendent and immanent, an idea that at its root wanted it both ways—God as absolute, another word for transcendent, and God as accepting of the contemporary relative sensibility. Such a view ultimately, though, will not work, as some process theologians acknowledge. So the workings of God—and thus God—are co-terminus with the workings of human relationship, of human creativity, of human struggles with "sameness" and "otherness" and the catastrophes and brilliances of trying to live together in a humane and nurturing world. As Cobb put it, where "creative human transformation" exists, there exists what we can call God. It is not that God is both "out there" and "down here" at the same time. It is that there is no God "out there," wherever out there is; God is only *here* where we humans live and work and have our being. God is in our "otherness" with each other. It may be more accurate to say that God is not *in* our mutual "otherness," but that God *is* our mutual "otherness." In a sense, that is the underlying assertion of most of today's process theology.

Symbolic interactionism is, in fact, related to process theology, since both had their origins at the same time around the University of Chicago, and symbolic interaction emerged as what I have called a "process sociology." When the idea of theology is added to symbolic interactionism, or process sociology—which I am doing, I think, for the first time here—it only emphasizes the immanence of the divine in the midst of the human, if divine there might be. The argument, in fact, would be that if there is to be anything of divinity in the affairs of the human species, it will be because humans learn to define each other in divine, or sacred, terms. While Christianity has much to contribute to the insights of such definitional processes, it is not the only religion interested in, or capable of, seeking such definitional categories. It, in fact, becomes the task of religion itself, whatever form it takes, to define and locate divinity; and "process sociology" would argue clearly that it must define and locate the divine spirit and nature in other human beings, whoever they be.

There is another contemporary theological movement, however, that finds some expression in what we have called for in preaching. It is a movement of what is generally called "narrative theology." It, too—at least in most of its expressions—is an extremely immanent form of theology, finding the "story of God" in the stories of humankind, and vice versa. Though I do not have the space here to explore this in detail, the beginnings of a concern with human "story" not long ago need to be connected here. In the mid-1970s, it was popular among homileticians to tell their seminary students that the most powerful preaching of the time was not that which took place in the pulpit, but the kind one found in the work of playwrights and novelists because, in Frederick Buechner's words, "it is often they better than the rest of us who speak with awful honesty about the absence of God in the world and about the storm of his absence."[11] It is, in other words, the makers of novels and plays who show us the human condition, who confront us with what we are like and how we treat each other. It is the makers of the world's stories who show us not only real ways in which we define each other, but the ways in which, under certain circumstances, we *might* define each other. In their work, we see ourselves in our full-blown encounters with those who stand in different places, who come into the present from a trail that we have never walked and can probably never know. But on the stage we meet; in the novel, we stand face-to-face.

All of this, for those homileticians, became a way to argue that seminarians—and preachers when they leave seminary—should be avid readers of novels and plays, should study and know the great narratives of our time. Such urgings, however, as accurate as they were, were sadly unrealistic. Preachers lacked, and still lack, the leisure for such reading; moreover, most preachers are not poets, nor do they have those rare abilities needed to grasp and bring novelistic processes into the pulpit. So preachers, even the good ones, turn phrases as best they can, while building their sermons around "issues"—social issues, ethical issues, theological issues. And issue-laden sermons, no matter how much we lace them with illustration and story, have a way of getting tedious. However, to begin to work from a preaching paradigm of "defining other," is, in a sense, to return to the common wisdom of homileticians who pushed novels and plays as pulpit models. Preaching from a stance of "defining the other," with all of its pluralistic ambiguities, is to put real faces on and behind one's sermons. It is to become an unrelenting student of human interaction, so that, from the pulpit, one becomes an ally to people who are struggling through those common, feverish, frustrating interactions. It is to become a sensitive absorber and processor of human outlook and perspective, and the interactions of those perspectives. It is to become a reflector and a leader in helping searching people come to terms with the new rhythms of life opened up by the unending new sets of definitions that pluralism makes not only possible but available.

This also opens up a way for us to see the gospel in a new light as well. It offers a way for us to develop a new "theology of gospel," in effect a process theology of gospel. The gospel is not some thing, nor is it a prescribed set of beliefs about something, or about anything. The gospel will be something that happens in human interaction, in the affairs of human beings acting toward each other, both as individuals in interactive situations and in collective situations. The gospel will be that which emerges as "grace" or as human "affirmation" in ways wholly unexpected and usually unpredictable. The idea of gospel itself is open-ended. When humans connect and embrace, particularly across divisive boundaries, when humans act toward each other, whatever their differences, with humility, with a sense of justice and concern, with a firm, intelligent, and sacrificial mutuality, there the gospel will poke through. What forms it will take, what ideas will be present in it, what religion will give it clarity, no one will be able to say in advance. It will be an "emergent" gospel. It will not be a "social gospel" in the old sense of that maligned term, but a social gospel in that it will represent grace in the healing of human conflict.

What the preacher is called on to do in this paradigm is assist in setting up the "conditions" under which the gospel might actually, from time to time, emerge in, across, and from the interactions, not just of parishioners themselves, but the interactions of parishioners with the larger, daily worlds in which they live and move. The preacher can assist with the searching and reformulating of definitions of "others." The preacher can provide a catalyst for "thinking through" old definitions—not just the narrow, often superior definitions of "us versus them," but the new definitions of people who live on the same block, people whose very presence so close often sets up fears, dreads, even hatreds within us. The world has changed, dramatically so, for everyone. We are surrounded by new cultures and new, sometimes explosive, mixtures of people, people both young and old. But who are they and where did they come from? What are we to do about them besides, perhaps, run? We need help in redefining them, help in determining not just who they are, but in saying who and what they will be to us in our definitional and behavior processes. The pluralist world in which we find ourselves is a world of new people, people who are not what we "remember," people who may have been somewhere all along, but now they are our—neighbors?

Ironically, this solves for the preacher the problem of whether to preach a "personal gospel" or a "social one," since this paradigm for the sermon virtually removes any such distinction. To work at new ways of defining the myriad of others—both interpersonal and collective—with whom one shares the world is both a very personal thing to do and a profoundly social activity as well. One must, from this perspective, work on one's own "faith," one's own definitional process; but that definitional process is itself not oriented toward oneself, but toward living as a new social creature in the larger social, political, ideological, economic, ethnic, sexual, and religious world.

At the same time, when we talk about the nature of "other" or "otherness" as a preaching paradigm, we are not talking about one kind of sermon among many kinds. Instead, what this suggests is that every sermon, whatever its topic or text or theological orientation, should address some dimension of human relationship, otherness. This is not the same as saying, as homileticians used to, that every sermon should have some "practical application," which no one would dispute; here, the contention is that every sermon should be designed, in some way, to help people define each other and the world's others in a more honoring, relational, embracing way, and that particular attention must continuously be given to those who are different from "us," however they are different, and whoever "us" is.

Preaching about "otherness," in short, is neither easy nor risk-free. Because it requires keen discernment and courage, it, too, may be understood as a new form of "prophetic preaching." Moreover, to preach of otherness, of our responsibility for others, or of how to define "God in others" who may stand for ideologies, sexual or gender orientations, and religions that are far from what we embrace, is to challenge our own views of those others, even as preachers. How do we define the other, either as an individual or a collective? To what extent have we subjected ourselves to the intense hub symbol scrutiny that we proposed in an earlier chapter, particularly a scrutiny of our sense of this particular other or that one? We are the ones, obviously, who must lead this process, who must cope with our own definitions of other before we can call others to do the same—even to join us in redefining all of the others with whom we share territory or community. Our own hub symbols will be deeply affected by this process, and we dare not let ourselves off the hook. We should use the best of our humane intellects, our tuned sensitivities, and our studies of both Bible and tradition—our own as well as those of other religions—to form new ways to define the multitude of others who make up this pluralistic world. We should then be encouraged to preach our own "revised" and "still-being-revised" hub symbols of "others." For us to engage in and urge others to share this process will not only create a new fermentation within our congregations; it may be the only way that, in the end, our congregations can become agents of a radically new gospel in a fiercely pluralistic world that still seems bent on destroying itself.

Appendix:
Exploring the Pluralist Sermon

This sermon is based on Luke 24:44–53, which was analyzed in Chapter 5. I have contended that the pluralist sermon is not one kind of sermon among many. Instead, I argue for a pluralist *perspective* on the sermon, a point of view that is brought to everything surrounding the sermon—to the text, to the sermon's objective, to its formation and desired outcome. The perspective is expressed, for the most part, in the questions one asks—the questions one continually asks—in going about the sermon-making process from week to week. Those questions are pluralist questions, questions related to defining one's own self and the relentless stream of "others" that impinge upon us, questions of harmonious living together in a tangled world of staggering human diversity. The preacher will quickly discover, however, that creating sermons from this perspective raises three crucial problems that must always be kept in mind. Briefly, I will call them problems of text, of theme and of tone.

The first is the problem of text. By that, I do not mean a problem of exegesis or analysis, which we have already considered, but a problem about what to do with the text, or one's conclusions about the text, *within* the sermon itself. This arises from the fact—as one can see from Chapter 5—that asking pluralist questions of a biblical text is often a troublesome thing to do. This is because so much in the Bible, including the New Testament, is not pluralist or even sympathetic to pluralism in the sense in which we have considered the nature of contemporary pluralism.[1] How does one even use a text, handled critically, in the sermon? Perhaps the text should be set aside, overlooked, or even ignored, as some preachers seem to do. This is in the spirit of "if you can't say anything nice about the text, don't say anything at all." But I don't think that is the answer. Neither is the answer to be found in constantly debunking texts, which can get very tiresome. What one can do in the sermon, however, is to "think through" a text with the congregants, to humanize the text, to ask where the text might have come from, what role it played within its community, and why it might, in fact, say or imply what it does. This is not a debunking activity as much as it is a de-mystifying one. It is a process not of putting the Bible down but of trying to understand it within its own setting, of letting the Bible, one might say, be human—as hard as such a statement might be for those who sanctify the Bible and biblical text. Ironically, contemporary people of all kinds are interested in the Bible, are interested in what it is, where it comes from, and why it makes the assertions it does. The preacher is in a position to "confront" the Bible, as it were, on behalf of congregants, treating it kindly, even reverently, but humanly, as a document from another time and place that needs to be de-sanctified.

The second problem to be dealt with in a pluralist sermon is its theme. What, in other words, will a sermon built upon or around this text be *about*? If one is simply willing to take the text, whatever it is, at face value, this is usually a fairly easy matter. The sermon is about Jesus' divinity; it is about forgiveness; it is about the need for self-sacrifice; it is about the warmth and security of community; it is about caring for the hungry of the world. But when one examines the text and, pluralistically, finds it wanting, *then* what will the sermon be about? The text will be implicitly *about* pluralism, about the pervasive problem of "otherness" and how we deal with "others" and how they "deal" with us. The text that we have from Luke, as I have handled it, is about a kind of pronounced "we-ness," so my concern in the sermon will be on the relationship between "we-ness" and "otherness." Ironically, the sermon in this case will not be about defining the "other," but about how "we" define ourselves and how others may very well define us *because* of how we might go about defining ourselves. My "theme," then, begins to take shape. In this case, I may use the sermon to ask questions: How do we define ourselves? And, how do others define *how* we define ourselves? Will I have the answers? Or even an answer? No, not really. But in yet another sense, probably yes. We will probably not know until the sermon is actually assembled and set down on paper in some way. Nevertheless, the overall intent of the sermon will be probing, exploratory, suggestive, prodding.

The third problem faced in the sermon from a pluralist perspective is that of tone. What may easily be described as a critical stance toward a text, such as the one that I have taken here, can translate itself into a critical sermon. This would give the sermon a slightly bitter flavor, a dark cast, a sense of being, some would say, a "downer." But that is not what we want. So one must work on the sermon's tone when devising a pluralist sermon. In working this particular text, one can take account of what I understand to be its negative side, something about which I can easily be critical: the attitude here at the end of Luke is flat-out arrogance. This is a community way beyond certainty in its own faith and understanding; it is a community of unabashed egos, of people who think more highly of themselves than they ought to think. Those thoughts are there for me. And yet—even though that may be gently said at some point—we will try to "understand" these people and turn the tone of the sermon into a positive one. This text, in my view, has at its heart a "danger," but one from which we can learn, a danger that offers us a much-needed caution. The people of this text are real people who can "speak to us" across time; and we can be in a position to listen, learn, and grow. The tone can be upbeat. The tone can be honest. The tone can be searching and forward-looking. But we must give close attention to the tone of what we say.

At this point, I am still not sure how the sermon itself will be fashioned, what its metaphorical framework will be. It could be "packaged" in any number of ways, using the direction on which I have set it so far. I have spent a lot of time over the past couple of years, though, studying the processes of "comedy," of humor. What gels in my mind, and connects to my thoughts about this text and this sermon is that "arrogance" is at the core of virtually all classical comedy. The stuffed shirt getting his—usually his—comeuppance is a staple of human comedy. My handling of this text wants to connect to that. I have an orientation now, even though there are still pieces to find and connections to make. But my track for the sermon is, for the most part, together. Here is the sermon that resulted from this process.

They Aren't Laughing at Us, Are They?
Read Luke 24: 44–53

In what is probably my favorite of the old MASH television episodes, Charles Winchester—you remember pompous old Charles, the aristocratic Boston medical doctor on MASH—Charles Winchester was looking forward to Christmas. And even though he was a long way from home, he was determined to keep a few of his old Bostonian Christmas traditions alive for himself even in the MASH unit camp. One of those traditions was that every Christmas from his boyhood years on, he would be treated—or he would treat himself—to a box of the finest, most expensive—meaning very expensive—chocolates that the most venerable Boston chocolatier had to offer. This Christmas would be no different. By long distance, he placed the order for his box of chocolates to be shipped to Korea. When they finally arrived, near Christmas, Winchester prepared for the ritual of eating the chocolates, one by one, thereby recreating for himself the memories of well-to-do Christmases past.

Strangely, though—and I recreate the MASH story in my memory, and my recollection may be off—Charles was struck by some twinge of Christmas conscience. He had seen the poverty of the region in which he found himself, particularly among the children; and he had seen it most visibly at the orphanage run by the nuns down the road from the MASH camp. Charles made a momentous Christmas decision. He would donate his box of Boston chocolates to the orphanage so that, for once in their lives, each child could be given a taste of the finest confection in the world. What a treat! It would be the least he could do for the unfortunates. With restrained, but unmistakable fanfare, he made the delivery of the box of chocolates to the nuns, giving them (as I recall) detailed instructions about both the origin of and process for handling the chocolates.

Christmas came and went, and when it was over word somehow came to Charles that the nuns had not given the chocolates to the children of the orphanage but, instead, had taken them into Seoul and sold them on the black market. In disbelief, Charles was utterly furious. He would confront the nuns and demand to know if—and why—they had so desecrated the Christmas gift that he had given to the children of the orphanage. He stormed—that's the way I remember it—he stormed the orphanage, pounded on the door until the nun in charge cracked it open. Enraged, Winchester demanded to know what had happened to the chocolates. She stepped outside in an effort to calm him down.

Yes, she reluctantly told him, the chocolates had not been given to the children, but had been taken into the city and sold.

Charles was beside himself with disbelief and blustery indignation.

"But," she said quietly, "the chocolates brought enough money in the city to feed every child in the orphanage for a full month."

It was a stunning piece of comedy. Or was it comedy? Of course it was. But what is comedic about it? What do we find ourselves laughing at, however quietly we laugh? There is, first of all, Winchester's attitude—without which there would be no comedy at all. It is his egotistical out-look, his cocky arrogance, his know-it-all-ness. It is his sureness, his rightness, or his *self*-rightness, his cultivated and unshakable view that he knows what is best, and that his sense of things should be everyone else's sense of things. He is a pompous ass, kind and gentle in so many ways; and yet his "better-than-thou" demeanor sets up the comic situation. But it doesn't become comic until someone—someone unexpected, someone "common," someone "beneath him," as it were—brings him down. Which is what the nun at the orphanage did. As we might say, she "gets him." She gives him what he deserves. She throws a pie in his face. And the "fall" that Winchester takes is the source of the comedy in the situation. It is classic comedy.

I say all this to ask if you will take a second look with me at the text we read a few moments ago, a different kind of look at it, really. It comes at the close of Luke's Gospel and it tells about Jesus leading the disciples out to the hill, giving them directions for what to do next and then going up, the text says, back to heaven. What it says is much more complex than that, of course. We don't know exactly when it was written, but many scholars place it in the '80s or so of the first century. That would mean it was written, from a variety of myths and legends, at least 50 years after Jesus' martyrdom. That's a long time. The story is not an eyewitness account—there is nothing wrong with us saying that. In fact, it doesn't even read like one. It is an imaginary story, drawn from various traditions or legends; one told, though, with purpose and vividness. The bottom line, though, is that this story, like the entire Gospel of Luke as well as the other Gospels, is a very important portrait of whoever wrote it, of the community from which it emerged. This is what my Claremont friend, James Sanders, an eminent scholar now retired, has called "canonical criticism." It is a view of the text, not as eyewitness history, but as a window, albeit a tiny, smudged window, into the workings and attitudes of those early communities of Christians out of which it came. So if we are really interested in what we might learn for ourselves and our time from those early Christian communities that shaped our pictures of Jesus, then we need to look *behind*—under, around, and behind—biblical texts like this one in order to explore who the people were, what they thought of each other, and what they thought of themselves, as reflected in their Jesus stories.

If we do that, if we even *try* to do that with this text at the end of Luke, we are confronted with both a fascinating and a disturbing notion. If we look closely at this text, at both its language and its implicit assertions, we—no, let me change the pronoun to I—when I look closely at this text, gently pulling it apart, or looking at it naively, which means trying to see it as though for the first time, I am struck with what I would describe initially as the *certainty* of these people. They have about them a flat-out confidence, or a sense of assurance. At least that is what it appears to be. They have, one might say, a confident faith of a very high order. And it is not so much a confidence about the event or events of the short episode. That's not it at all. Nor is it just a confident faith in who Jesus was, however they have learned about Jesus. That is part of it, but that it not the root of their confidence. It is, instead, a confidence about *who and what they are,* the people in the story. And the story they write about the past, about Jesus and those disciples back then, is *their* story; *that* is what they are absolutely certain about. The exclusive position that Jesus, God's representative, gave to those disciples back then, he has also, by extension, given to them. They are the heirs of a very special, and very exclusive, heritage. Of that, they are certain. To say the least, there is a fascinating and important psychology going on here.

The text has a subtext of assertions or affirmations. Can you hear what they are? Listen, or follow down the text yourself as I go through them. We are the ones—the disciples of Jesus then, and "us" in the present, since we are their heirs—we are the ones who have been given the secrets of the ancient writings. We are the ones who are now the true interpreters of the writings of Moses, of the prophets, and even the psalms. We are the ones who have seen all of those ancient scriptures completely fulfilled. We are the ones who have made our minds opened to understand the scriptures. We are the ones who are now prepared to call all peoples everywhere to repentance. We are the ones designated to mete out forgiveness of sins on behalf of God. We are the ones who are now sent to all nations to turn them to God. We are the chosen witnesses to the ultimate work of God for all time. We are the ones whom Jesus, the very offspring of God, chose to bless. We are the ones who have been clothed with power—what a remarkable image—from on high. We are the ones who were commissioned. We are the ones who can lead others in, as the text says, blessing God. We are the ones. We are the ones. In this Lukan text, the announcement is made. We are the ones. And we are also the writers of the announcement.

There is no desire here to make this remarkable biblical text out to be something that it isn't. And there may be good reason, based on the time and circumstance of Luke's Gospel, for drawing self-confident and unmistakable lines in the sand—as this text does. Some scholars point out that any new movement must clearly separate itself from other movements, and this requires a kind of aggressive overstatement. I take nothing away from what those reasons might be. But the fact remains that there is a severe *danger* lurking in how this text is formed, a danger that we might be able to account for or even justify by setting the text in time and place. But it is a danger nonetheless, particularly if subsequent generations take the absoluteness and exclusivity of this text as applying as well to themselves. Which, history tells us, is what the church tended to do over the following centuries—and even does right down to the present.

The outcome was not just a benign confidence among these people in their own calling, in their own power from God to be the once-and-for-all light shining in the world of darkness. Confidence is good. A sureness about what one believes and about one's own standing before God is to be desired and applauded. But there is a dangerous line. And the line is between confidence and arrogance. If this text from Luke does not reflect an implicit arrogance—and I am afraid that it does—then the church's subsequent leaders turned the text's confidence into arrogance, often an ugly and violent arrogance—as numerous eras in the church's two-thousand year history make all too clear.

But what if we reflect on ourselves in light of this text and what I take to be a kind of swagger in it? We—yes, you and I—are we the ones whose minds God has opened? Are we the ones, and not those other religious folk, those folk who grew up in other religions, even other religions that are not Christian? Are they the ones with the closed minds while ours, thank God, are the ones that have been opened? Are we the ones picked by God to be the "keepers of truth," truth that was embodied in—and only in—Jesus Christ? Are we the ones who, by God's grace and mercy, have been blessed with power from on high—power, of course, that has come to us by the Holy Spirit's work upon us? We? Us? It has an odd sound about it if we are not careful, doesn't it? It is not something that we might even find ourselves saying out loud. But do we think it? Is it what we have been taught to believe?

In all honesty, it is what I grew up with, the child of a preacher's family. A devout family, reasoned and gentle in every way. An educated Christian family that cared deeply about others and that taught us four children the values of all that. But we were a Christian family, and my dad preached intensely and unequivocally the unique, God-given finality of the Christian faith. We did not wonder who God's elect were. We were, and those who were not like us religiously were lost, if their religion was not Christianity, or were suspect, if they were not our particular brand of Protestant. I mean no disrespect to my family or its faith—I am deeply grateful for it. But I am trying to get it into perspective. While my father probably never said so specifically from the pulpit, he certainly preached and taught the ultimate superiority and exclusivity of Christianity. This was not *a* religion. It was *the* religion. The only *true* religion of God. Religiously, it was the largest sheaf of wheat, the one to which all the other sheaves had to bow down. We grew up with it. It was inculcated within us, at least within me. It was shaken a few times, but not until I got to graduate school. Yet not even then, really, since I was determined to go into the ministry. I had a "mission" in the world, a mission to Christianize it. And it was not so much cultural—I see, looking back—as it was religious, theological.

In my late twenties, I left the Midwest and headed west to my first teaching job in California, where I was assigned to share an office with another new faculty member, a Ph.D. fresh out of USC. My new friend Sam was Jewish, reformed but devout. He knew and loved his Judaism, and he was as fascinated to be up close to a full-fledged Protestant evangelical as I was to be up close, for the first time, to a full-fledged Jew who sometimes wore his yarmulke cap. We talked. Or rather, I talked some. Mostly I listened. We explored faith, our faiths, together. My view of faith changed. My view of religion changed. My view of myself and my faith changed. It was not my faith that changed, really. It was my view of how faith was perceived and held by others. It was a crash course for me— some will find it strange that it took me so long, or that I had not known such things all along. But I didn't. There were, I finally grasped, other profoundly held faiths in the world, faiths other than mine. Mine was my faith, and, even tested in the fire of larger religious worlds, I could hold it with dignity and meaning. But I realized that my saying that meant that others of other faiths could also say it about their faith. Could we learn from each other? Yes, I learned that we could. It was no longer possible to see myself or my faith as inherently superior to that of Sam, or others.

Not long ago, I encountered an article in a journal that crossed my desk, an article by a Christian woman from India. It was a scholarly discussion of the Great Commission, Matthew 28: 18–20, the text that is the counterpart to the one that we read earlier, counterpart in the sense that it concludes the Gospel of Matthew, just as ours concludes Luke's Gospel. You remember its words, attributed to Jesus: "Go therefore and make disciples of all nations, …teaching them to obey everything I have commanded you. And remember I am with you always, even to the end of the age." It is the text that has fired the Christian missionizing of the world virtually from Christianity's beginning 2,000 years ago. The author of the article described the Christian missionaries in India during her growing up, their view of the heathen masses there; and she called the commission in Matthew a "text of terror." This woman of India, whose name is Ivy George, described the Great Commission as—and these are her words— a manifesto for violence against peoples and cultures outside the parochial boundaries of traditional Western Christianity. She became a Christian in her youth but now looks back at it in order to come to terms with Christianity as a religion in the world. As such, she makes a plea in her essay for an *end* to Christian missionizing of the world. Instead of that, she urges that Christians learn to live with other peoples of all religions who are, as she says, *committed to granting of dignity and the minimizing of violence in human interaction with the universe.* A remarkable statement.

What we are faced with, you and I, is not a first-century world, not a fifth- or a twelfth-century world, but a twenty-first century one. And it is a world, as you well know, that has grown astoundingly small. Its smallness means that we know each other on this planet remarkably well, far better than the peoples of the planet have ever known each other before. We know each other's cultures, often up close and personal. We know each other's ways of thinking, whether we like those ways of thinking or not. We know each other's religious beliefs—maybe not in detail—but we know them. And we know that we all have our own histories, too, histories of race and belief and ideology and religion. We know. And we all know, down deep, the limitations that make us human, no matter who we are. We are, in a sense, all in this together. And, religiously, the one thing this new world of the twenty-first century cannot afford is arrogance. Not from this religion or that one, not from this sect or some other—and certainly not from Christians. This means that we cannot afford—or, rather, our world cannot afford—for us any longer to believe, or preach, that we are the only true religion, the only religion authorized by God, the only religion through which God has sent divine power upon earth.

We can be confident that our faith in God is our faith in God, that it is not only satisfying to us within the depth of our souls, but that it has historical roots that we claim to give it form and substance. But if that confidence turns into arrogance, then we have passed from the humility of Christ to the haughtiness of the Pharisees, as the Christians came to caricature them. We have turned our Christianity into Winchesterism.

When I was much younger—back in the 1960s, in fact—I was fascinated, as some of you probably were, with Lenny Bruce, the notorious comedian who died in 1966. I never saw him in person, but recordings of his act certainly made the rounds when I was in graduate school at the University of Illinois. I was both troubled and fascinated with, shall we say, the blueness of his work. But that wasn't what caught my ear about Lenny Bruce back in those days. What caught my ear was the fact that no one used humor, comedy, to deal with *religion*, particularly Christianity, more than he did. For some of us—I was among them—he was a legal target not so much for his verbal obscenity—that was a factor, of course—but for his attacks on the church, and not just the Roman Catholic Church, but on organized Christianity in all of its forms. His attacks were brutal and, I am sad to say, uproariously funny. They were funny precisely because of the arrogance of church leaders who believed that they were God on earth, that when they spoke, God spoke. They were Winchester in their collars and vestments—and Lenny Bruce threw pie all over them.

I still vividly remember sitting around with two or three dozen other guys in a rooming house where I lived while the tape player blared Bruce's routine about Jesus and Moses showing up at St. Pat's Cathedral while

Cardinal Spellman held forth in the pulpit. No graduate-student studying was going on that night. There was nothing but the most raucous laughter as Bruce unloaded on the clergy. I still have the dog-eared verbatim copy of the routine that circulated after that night.

In Lenny Bruce's monologue, it was Bishop Fulton J. Sheen—that name will not mean anything to many of you here, but he was the best-known TV clergyman of that era—Bishop Sheen went to the pulpit and tried to interrupt Spellman to tell him that he was not going to believe it, but there were two familiar-looking guys nosing around at the back of the church. "They're here! They're here!" Sheen kept saying to Spellman, trying to get his attention. "They're standing at the back now," Sheen said; "don't look now, you idiot"—this is Bruce's routine—"they can see us."

"Which ones are they?" Spellman finally asks Sheen.

"The ones that're glowing," Sheen replies, with a "Hoo! Glowing! Terrible!"

"Are you sure it's them?" Spellman asks.

"I've seen 'em in pictures," Sheen replies, "but I'm pretty sure—Moses is a ringer for Charlton Heston."

"Are they armed?" Spellman wants to know.

"I dunno," Sheen answers.

"Poor box locked?" Spellman asks.

"Yeah. I'll grab the box and meet you round the back!" Sheen says.

"No, we better cool it," Spellman says. "You better get me Rome, quickly. Now what the hell do they want here?"

"Maybe," Sheen says, "they want to audit the books?"

It goes on much longer. And not only that, but within the next few lines of Bruce's monologue, a group of lepers show up following Christ and Moses into the church. That's when things really get tough for Cardinal Spellman. Protestant clergy are brought onto the scene in Bruce's monologue. It is loud and boisterous, and the pompous church and its pompous clergy are lambasted from every conceivable direction. For a religious person listening to it still, one doesn't know whether to laugh or cry. It was all about arrogance. The arrogance of the church, or the churches, or the clergy or…whomever. I'm not sure.

It is no longer polite, or politically correct, to do what Lenny Bruce did as far as religion is concerned. Not many comedians are up to letting religion have it anymore. They—we—laughed at Christianity. Not at Christianity so much as at a Christianity that got too big for its britches, a Christianity that believed that it alone was the road to heaven for all people of all time in all situations—a Winchester Christianity. There is the simple nun, of course, and that is who we probably ought to be. But how much are we the nun, we who claim to be Christian; and how much are we Winchester? Is it a fair question? Is it? They aren't laughing at us now, are they?

The nature and design of this sermon is not, as some might suggest, an isolated process. There are, of course, many New Testament texts to be affirmed, particularly Gospel texts, and what is said here is to take nothing away from those texts. Yet, with text upon text, when one asks pluralist questions and works pluralistically through a text, one is confronted with the need to think with a critical heart and mind—not with a negative criticalness, but with a positive one, one from which the church of today can and must learn. For those interested in other textual studies from which I have preached other sermons like "They Aren't Laughing at Us, Are They?" one may consult "Deconstruction/Reconstruction: New Preaching from Old Texts," *Quarterly Review* 16/4 (Winter 1996): 425–50. These lectionary studies also deal with John 17: 6–19, John 15: 26–27; John 16: 4b–15; and John 3: 1–17.

Notes

INTRODUCTION
The Dimensions of the "New Pluralism"

[1] (Philadelphia: Westminster, 1975). Cobb is the author of numerous works, though he is best known as the parent of "process theology," which continues to exert wider and wider influence from its base at the Claremont School of Theology.

[2] Cobb, 58.

[3] In 1987, when homiletician David Buttrick published his magnum opus on preaching (*Homiletic: Moves and Structures*, Philadelphia: Fortress, 1987), only one paragraph in his entire book of almost 500 pages was devoted to pluralism.

[4] The reasons for the swift reconfiguring of the world's populations are very complex, of course, but no one can look back over the history of the twentieth century and doubt the seminal roles played by changes in the technologies of interaction and movement. Studies on the effects of mass communication particularly, abound. As early as the mid-1920s, an eminent sociologist, to whom we shall turn again shortly, was able to comment: "The easy means of communication and transportation, which enable individuals to distribute their attention and to live at the same time in several different worlds, tend to destroy the permanency and intimacy of the neighborhood. On the other hand, the isolation of the immigrant and racial colonies of the so-called ghettoes and areas of population segregation tend to preserve, and, where there is racial prejudice, to intensify the intimacies and solidarities of the local and neighborhood groups" (Robert E. Park, "The City: Suggestions for the Investigation of Human Behavior in the Urban Environment," from *The City*, edited by Park and Ernest W. Burgess [Chicago: University of Chicago Press, 1925], 9).

[5] I know this from my own experience as pastor of a small church in suburban Los Angeles. Our congregation of a few dozen people owned a large church building (in the 1960s, before the town's steel mills closed, it was a large congregation), and we leased the facilities to a large Korean congregation. What should have been a happy relationship was often filled with tension, since the Korean congregation cooked "foreign" food, including kimchee, every week in the church kitchen. Language, too, was a problem, since we did not speak Korean and many of the Koreans did not speak English. How to speak to each other? And our much smaller group often felt overwhelmed by the large numbers of the Korean congregation. We managed—we needed the income—but the interaction was often problematic. Every situation is different,

of course, and in many places the American congregation is larger and probably less intimidated by the sharing congregation.

[6] The use of these two models—the elephant one and the collision one—arise from the theories of journalism and communication that were widely discussed twenty-five to thirty years ago. Then there was "old," or so-called objective journalism, which operated on the elephant model, and the emergence of what came to be known as "new journalism," which rejected the notion of consensual objectivity and dealt with the idea that perspectives on anything had a life and a validity of their own. Many of us at that time—my first two decades of teaching were in journalism and communication environments—explored at length the implications of this change. See my book *Writing the New Journalism* (New York: Richards Rosen, 1977) for an exploration of these models in another context.

[7] The relation between process theology and the University of Chicago at the turn into the twentieth century is well documented. A subsection of a long Appendix in Cobb and Griffin's *Process Theology: An Introductory Exposition* is called "Process Theology: The Chicago School," and it begins: "The major center of theological receptivity to Whitehead's influence was the Divinity School of the University of Chicago. Indeed, process theology can trace its history almost as well through this school as to Whitehead. What is today called process theology is largely the result of the way Whitehead's influence, along with the teaching of Charles Hartshorne, modified the thought of members of this school" (176). Ironically, the dates for the formation of process theology at Chicago extend from about 1895 through the early 1930s, paralleling George Herbert Mead's role in social psychology at the University of Chicago.

[8] Even though historical essays on these early sociological developments can be found in numerous places, particularly as introductory pieces when the original materials were republished after 1960, no scholar has probed more carefully or insightfully into the history, significance, and origins of the Chicago school than Hugh Dalziel Duncan. See, in particular, Duncan's *Communication and Social Order* (New York: Oxford University Press, 1962) and *Symbols and Social Theory* (New York: Oxford University Press, 1969).

[9] The terms here are usually credited to Robert Park, who used them in his essay "The Romantic Temper," in *The City*, 119.

[10] See Park, "The Neighborhood," in *The City*, 146.

[11] Of all of these writings, Morris Janowitz noted in 1967 as the republishing of these materials was underway: "These men wrote of magic and mentality; they sought to describe myth and intellectuality. They were sociologists who realized that the tradition, custom, and romantic aspirations of city dwellers converted ecological, economic and industrial factors into a social organization. In their search for objectivity and generality they did not find it necessary to deny a concern with the values that propel human beings. It is for this reason they often used the term social organization; to organize implies that men are creating social values and social goals." See *The City*, 1967 edition, ix.

[12] The classic methodological statement of this era, one that, in many ways, shaped the tradition and American sociology itself, is by W. I. Thomas, who was joined by Florian Znaniecki. It is the first 80 pages of *The Polish Peasant in America*, simply called "Methodological Note." It has been reprinted in several places, including Znaniecki's book *On Humanistic Sociology* (Chicago: University of Chicago Press, 1969).

13 Heinz Maus, *A Short History of Sociology* (Princeton: Princeton University Press, 1961), 122.

14 Duncan, *Symbols and Social Theory*, xvii.

15 Park, "Spatial Pattern and Moral Order," 67.

16 Throughout Mead's writings are notes and analyses of Whitehead's work. One will find a section, for example, in Volume 3 of Mead's *The Philosophy of the Act* (Chicago: University of Chicago Press, 1938), titled "Fragments on Whitehead."

17 Duncan, *Symbols and Social Theory*, 197.

18 Ibid.

CHAPTER ONE
Symbolicity: Why We See Things Differently

1 Langer, *Philosophical Sketches* (Baltimore: Johns Hopkins University Press, 1962). Through Cassirer, Langer was influenced by Mead and the symbolic interactionists, though she came at it from an aesthetic viewpoint. Everywhere one reads in Langer, though, one finds her adapting this symbolic perspective to art and the "logic" of art.

2 See Leslie A. White, *The Science of Culture: A Study of Man and Civilization* (New York: Farrar, Strauss and Giroux, 1949), 25.

3 Cassirer, *An Essay on Man* (New Haven, Connecticut: Yale University Press, 1944): "That symbolic thought and symbolic behavior are among the most characteristic features of human life, and that the whole progress of human culture is based on these conditions, is undeniable" (27). At another point, Cassirer notes that the "animal possesses a practical imagination and intelligence whereas man alone has developed a new form: a symbolic imagination and intelligence" (33).

4 See Kenneth Burke, *Language as Symbolic Action: Essays on Life, Literature and Method* (Berkeley: University of California Press, 1968), 5.

5 Mead defined the "significant symbol," which virtually occupied all of his thinking about the nature of symbolism, as anything that called out in one person what it called out in others. What others, and recent communications scholars in particular, have made clear in their studies of symbolism from the symbolic interactionist perspective is that the symbol not only can be but often is highly idiosyncratic; in fact, as we shall see in the next chapter, the essence of creativity—and of social deviance—is the ability to devise one's own symbols.

6 This viewpoint emerged during the early 1930s largely as a result of a book by Alfred Korzybski, a mathematician and engineer, titled *Science and Sanity* (New York: Dutton, 1933). The book's concern was how to bring a deeply divided planet back together again, and its "solution" was to create a "value-free" language sytem, a neutral language, one free of all emotional content or overtones. It represented a return to a Platonic philosophy which said that somewhere there is a "real elephant" and a "real tree," and if we could just find the right words we could "see" it all in some pure and unified way again. Ironically, this view, too, exerted an influence on homiletics. One can find it, for example, in a book by James Daane titled *Preaching With Confidence: A Theological Essay on the Power of the Pulpit* (Grand Rapids, Mich.: Eerdmans, 1980).

There Daane wrote:

> Contemporary life is full of examples of this reduction of language to our subjective determination....Words were like x's in an algebraic equation, having no inherent meaning but only standing for what was determined by the composer of the equation. It is no wonder that for people today, disillusioned by countless cases like this, the power of words to communicate has broken down....When the nexus between language and reality has been broken and words cut loose from their mooring and cast adrift, so that the meaning of language is up for grabs, everyone is eligible to be his own Webster....We can communicate with each other only if the meaning of our words derives from their relationship to reality. Without such a common point of reference our words pass each other like ships in the night. When this occurs community breaks down, for community depends upon communication and communication depends on consensus as to the meaning of words. (18, 19)

[7] Burke's most comprehensive statement of this is in his essay "Semantic and Poetic Meaning," in *The Philosophy of Literary Form* (New York: Vintage, 1941). There he writes:

> The difference between the semantic ideal and the poetic ideal of moralistic interpretation would, I think, get down to this: The semantic ideal would attempt to get a description by the elimination of attitude. The poetic ideal would attempt to attain a full moral act by attaining a perspective atop the conflicts of attitude. The first would try to cut away, to abstract, all emotional factors that complicate the objective clarity of meaning. The second would try to derive its vision from the maximum heaping up of all these emotional factors, playing them off against one another, inviting them to reinforce and contradict each other, and seeking to make this active participation itself a major ingredient of the vision. (128)

One finds this idea everywhere, in fact, in Burke. See a number of his essays in *Language as Symbolic Action: Essays in Life, Literature and Method* (Berkeley: University of California Press, 1968), particularly "Poetics in Particular, Language in General," "Terministic Screens," and "Rhetoric and Poetics."

[8] Burke says this in many ways and places throughout his writing. For example, one comment must suffice: "Our philosophers, poets, and scientists act in the code of names by which they simplify or interpret reality. These names shape our relations with our fellows. They prepare us for some functions and against others, for or against the persons representing these functions. The names go further: they suggest how you shall be for or against. Call a man a villain, and you have the choice of either attacking or cringing. Call him mistaken, and you invite yourself to attempt setting him right." See *Attitudes Toward History* (Boston: Beacon, 1937), 4.

[9] See White, "The Symbol: The Origin and Basis of Human Behavior," in *The Science of Culture*. White points out that the same thing may, in some cases, function both as a symbol and a sign, but he is clear about making a difference between the two. White writes:

> The man differs from the dog—and all other creatures—in that he can and does play an active role in determining what value the vocal stimulus is to have, and the dog cannot....Whether (the dog) is to roll over or go

fetch at a given stimulus, or whether the stimulus for roll over be one combination of sounds or another is a matter in which the dog has nothing whatever to "say." He plays a purely passive role and can do nothing else. He learns the meaning of a vocal command just as his salivary glands may learn to respond to the sound of a bell. But man plays an active role and thus becomes a creator (with symbols): let x equal three pounds of coal and it does equal three pounds of coal; let removal of the hat in a house of worship indicate respect and it becomes so. This creative faculty, that of freely, actively, and arbitrarily bestowing value upon things, is one of the most commonplace as well as the most important characteristics of man. (29)

[10] See Burke, "Definition of Man," the opening essay in *Language as Symbolic Action: Essays on Life, Literature and Method* (Berkeley: University of California Press, 1968), 4.

[11] Cassirer, *An Essay on Man*, 84, 85.

[12] Ibid., 25.

[13] My colleague Kathy Black of the Claremont School of Theology faculty, who has done considerable work among the deaf, makes clear throughout her writing that the hearing parents of deaf children cannot teach signing language to their children, nor can deaf parents of hearing children teach those children "their" language. By the same token, in such families the children do not just pick up the language of their parents. This represents an exception to the rule of language-learning, however, wherein children who are like their parents pick up the parental language as a matter of "normal" development.

[14] David Buttrick, *Homiletic: Moves and Structures* (Philadelphia: Fortress, 1987), 179, 180.

[15] Burke, for example, devotes an enormous amount of space to the unique powers of language, even while treating language as one of many symbol systems. Few essays on language in this century carry the power of Burke's "Terministic Screens" found in his book *Language as Symbolic Action: Essays on Life, Literature and Method* (Berkeley: University of California Press, 1966). His argument is summed up, for example, in this statement:

> We must use terministic screens, since we can't say anything without the use of terms; whatever terms we use, they necessarily constitute a corresponding kind of screen; and any such screen necessarily directs the attention to one field rather than another. Within that field there can be different screens, each with its ways of directing the attention and shaping the range of observations implicit in a given terminology. All terminologies must implicitly or explicitly embody choices between the principle of continuity and the principle of discontinuity. (50)

[16] Charles Keil, *Urban Blues* (Chicago: University of Chicago Press, 1966).

CHAPTER TWO
Defining: Why We Act In Different Ways

[1] These researchers did come up with a few basic notions which they tended to verify, even though they could not be held to be discoveries, as such; for example, that subjects tended to change their opinions more if the direction to do so came from a

"high credibility" source than if it came from a "low credibility" source. And, that messages designed to "arouse fear" could, in fact, arouse fear, except when they became excessive, at which point the messages themselves were simply rejected. They also discovered that arguments for a message that came first or last in a list were more persuasive than arguments in the middle of a list, even though it was difficult to predict whether the first or the last message would prove most persuasive; these became known as the "primacy-recency" studies. Most of these studies were psychologically-oriented, even though this tradition also had its sociology side. One can find summaries of this research in many places, particularly in anthologies of communications theory and research. For example, one may turn to an excellent series of articles in Kenneth K. Sereno and C. David Mortensen (eds.), *Foundations of Communication Theory* (New York: Harper and Row, 1970). See, in particular, Irvin L. Janis and Carl I. Hovland, "An Overview of Persuasibility Research." Janis and Hovland were two of the key figures in this research, themselves publishing several books of their findings, such as *Personality and Persuasibility* (New Haven: Yale University Press, 1959), and *Communication and Persuasion: Psychological Studies of Opinion Change* (New Haven: Yale University Press, 1953).

[2] William I. Thomas, *The Unadjusted Girl* (Boston: Little, Brown, 1931). The concept was more elaborately described in a massive work by Thomas and Florian Znaniecki, titled *The Polish Peasant in Europe and America* (Boston: Richard G. Badger, 1918–1920; Vols. 1 and 2 originally published by the University of Chicago Press, 1918).

[3] Various parts of Thomas' work considered the process by which symbols or definitions are "learned," beginning with the family, which he dubbed the "primary group." At one point, for example, he writes:

> The family is the smallest social unit and the primary defining agency. As soon as the child has free motion and begins to pull, tear, pry, meddle, and prowl, the parents begin to define the situation through speech and other signs and pressures: 'Be quiet,' 'Sit up straight,' 'Blow your nose,' 'Wash your face,' 'Mind your mother,' 'Be kind to sister,' etc. This is the real significance of Wordsworth's phrase, 'Shades of the prison house begin to close upon the growing child.' His wishes and activities begin to be inhibited, and gradually, by definitions within the family, by playmates, in the school, in the Sunday School, in the community, through reading, by formal instruction, by informal signs of approval and disapproval, the growing member learns the code of his society. (42)

[4] Such learning, though, is not just coincidental. In many cases, definitions are "forged" out of shared experience. For example, in one of the most famous studies of social behavior, Howard Becker in the early 1960s analyzed how a young person could become a marijuana user, an action that is both illegal and not inherently—as he pointed out—pleasurable (see "Becoming a Marijuana User," in *Outsiders: Studies in the Sociology of Deviance*, New York: Free Press, 1963). Becker worked from within the symbolic interactionist tradition, meaning that he rejected psychological reasons for marijuana use; it was not used, he argued, for fantasy reasons or as a means of escaping from psychological problems. Instead, he argued that marijuana use arose from social forces pulling on young people who, in turn, learned to "define" marijuana and the experience of using it in collective, pleasurable terms.

[5] Thomas, 42. It was, in fact, the understanding of this principle of the "definition of the situation" that stood in such stark contrast earlier in the century to the behavioral

models in social psychology that saw human behavior in stimulus-response terms. What Thomas explicitly introduced into the human behavioral equation—and in an experimental, "scientific" fashion—was the problem of subjectivity. Human behavior cannot be understood by focusing on external events or circumstances, but only by grasping the symbolic process of how a subject defines a situation. Also incorporated into this concept was what Thomas called the "power of inhibition," by which he meant the ability of the human to refuse to accept a stimulus. If something were done to one that caused pain, then the next time the same circumstance presented itself, a person could refuse to accept the circumstance again. If one symbolized a situation as causing a problem, that symbol could be called up to change behavior in the same or a similar situation; that, in fact, is what happened in the case of the person who ran from our fictitious room.

6 Mead, as Kenneth Burke said of him, provided the crucial shift from a romantic view of Self to a realistic one, a shift that was based on his remarkably new sense of the mind. In Burke's words, "The strategy of romantic philosophy (which Mead likens to the beginnings of self-consciousness at adolescence) was to identify the individual Self metaphysically with the Absolute Self, thereby making the reflexive act the very essence of the universe, a state of affairs open to lewd caricature. But Mead, turning from a metaphysical emphasis to a sociological one, substitutes for the notion of the Absolute Self the notion of mind as a social product, stressing the sociability of action and reflection, and viewing thought as the internalization of objective relationships" (*Philosophy of Literary Form*, 308).

7 Troyer, in Jerome Manis and Bernard Meltzer (eds.), *Symbolic Interaction: A Reader in Social Psychology* (Chicago: Allyn and Bacon, 1982), 324.

8 See White, "Mind is Minding," in *Science of Culture*, 52. After discussing the long-standing problem of the mind and body dichotomy, White adds: "By rewording the problem, the 'problem' disappears: use the word 'mind' as a verb instead of a noun and no 'problem,' fundamental either to the theory of knowledge, ethics, psychology, science or anything else, remains. Mind is minding; it is the behaving, reacting, of a living organism of a whole, as a unit" (50).

9 We can only try to summarize in a short space here what is, in Mead's writing, elaborated thoroughly. The most concise orientation to it is in the first of three sections of his "book"—in quotation marks since the book was assembled from his work—titled *Mind, Self and Society*, edited by Charles W. Morris (Chicago: University of Chicago Press, 1934, 1962).

CHAPTER THREE
Hub Symbols: Why Our Differences Become So Volatile

1 In *Permanence and Change* (Indianapolis: Bobbs-Merrill, 1935), Burke called this "piety." With grace and simplicity, he sketched it like this: "Piety is a system-builder, a desire to round things out, to fit experiences together into a unified whole. Piety *is the sense of what properly goes with what* (his emphasis)....Piety is a scheme of orientation, since it involves the putting together of experiences. The orientation may be right or wrong; it can guide or misguide. If the bird saw an actual danger, the flock was right in rising with it. If the danger was not real, the flock was wrong. In either case it had been pious" (74-76).

2 *Permanence and Change*, 74.

[3] Not coincidentally, another group of researchers in the late 1950s and 1960s were also working on symbolicity, but from what they considered a more scientific orientation. They were led by Charles Osgood and Martin Fishbein. Along with other colleagues, they devised and refined what they called the "semantic differential," a research tool that became a standard in communications research. At the heart of semantic differential theory—influenced by symbolic interactionism—is the idea that every concept (i.e., symbol) is essentially defined by the degree and direction of its emotional content, or, more specifically, by the amount and direction of the emotion placed in the concept by someone who uses it. The semantic differential research design was implemented as a means of measuring the amount of emotion that one invested in a given concept or statement. One will find this in its original discussion in the book by Osgood, George Susi, and Percy Tannenbaum, *The Measurement of Meaning* (Urbana: University of Illinois Press, 1957).

[4] The very idea of "primary group" is a product of the early symbolic interactionist tradition, ascribed usually to Charles Horton Cooley. See Cooley's book, *Social Organization* (New York: Schocken Books, 1909, reprinted, Scribner's, 1967). The tradition of work, however, on primary and family groups in symbolic interactionism has been consistent for many years. One need only read two essays which appear in the 1982 edition of Manis and Meltzer to see the work on "primary groups": Sheldon Stryker's "Symbolic Interaction as an Approach to Family Research" and William R. Rosengren's "The Self in the Emotionally Disturbed."

[5] One may detect some similarity between this orientation and Paul Tillich's famous notion of faith as "ultimate concern." While Tillich speaks of the role of symbols in that ultimate concern, it is not with the understanding of "symbol" that has been developed here. His is a far more metaphysical view of symbol, even though he argues that there is, within the human psyche, a center and that whatever is in that center represents the ultimate concern of the individual. Tillich writes at one point that "the ultimate concern gives depth, direction and unity to all other concerns and, with them, to the whole personality. A personal life which has these qualities is integrated, and the power of a personality's integration is his faith" (See *Dynamics of Faith* [New York: Harper & Row, 1957], 107).

CHAPTER FOUR
Pluralism and the Bible: Preaching and the Symbolism of the Book

[1] The history summarized briefly here is told at length in many places. In my judgment, one of the best tellings of the story is Catherine L. Albanese's *America: Religions and Religion* (Belmont: Wadsworth, 1992).

[2] The backgrounds and extended discussions of what is only sketched here can be found in numerous places. The cleavage discussed here is what turned the attention of the finest theologians of the mid-twentieth century to the dilemma of "revelation," that is, to the issues surrounding the authority and nature of the Bible and how it figures in one's understanding of God. As George Stroup put it in 1981: "During the first half of the twentieth century, Protestant theology, especially that movement loosely labeled 'neo-orthodoxy,' made revelation the systematic principle for the elucidation of the other doctrines of the Christian faith. Books such as the first two volumes of Karl Barth's *Church Dogmatics*, Emil Brunner's *Revelation and Reason*, and

H. Richard Niebuhr's *The Meaning of Revelation* are evidence of the preoccupation with revelation by theologians during the 1930s and 1940s." See George W. Stroup, *The Promise of Narrative Theology: Recovering the Gospel in the Church* (Atlanta: John Knox, 1981), 39-42.

3 Thousands of pages have been written about Karl Barth's influence on twentieth century theology and wherever one reads in Barth's highly-varied writings, one finds a kind of lament about the loss of the Bible in the pulpit. One also finds a constant effort and plea to let the Bible be the Bible for preaching; let the Bible be the Word of God without human wrangling or embellishment: It is Barth's great song, nowhere given more effective voice than in his own lectures on homiletics. In his foreword to the 1991 publication of those lectures, David Buttrick summed up Barth's relation to these issues:

> Probably Barth has been criticized most for his strong, uncompromising biblicism: so strong that he is willing to suggest that preachers risk no more than a "reiteration" of the text lest, in interpreting, they admix the scripture's message with their own cultural thoughts. "The sermon," he suggests, "will be like the involuntary lip movement of one who is reading with great care, attention, and surprise." Barth clings to scripture, guards scripture fiercely, and will allow no dilution of scripture's divine Word. Because of his stubborn reverence for the Bible, Barth has been embraced enthusiastically by many moderating fundamentalists in recent years. He is unabashedly biblical and seems to have had no awareness of the "hermeneutic problem" that within a quarter of a century would agitate the theological community (foreword to Karl Barth, *Homiletics* [Louisville: Westminster/John Knox, 1991], 9).

4 Among the many books like this that appeared, particularly during the 1960s, none was more interesting and insightful than the one by the great German preacher Helmut Thielicke, *The Trouble With the Church* (Grand Rapids: Baker, 1965). Thielicke spoke from within the church about the decline of preaching—he called it the "plight of preaching" in his opening pages—so his book hit home in its combination of the practical problems of such things as credibility and boredom, along with his scholarly sense of how the Bible itself had fallen out of the process.

5 Leander Keck, *The Bible in the Pulpit* (Nashville: Abingdon, 1978). He put the issue clearly:

> Historical thinking means perceiving things in historical relationships, as part of the stream of events and factors that conditions everything. Historical thinking understands things in light of continuities and developments, antecedents and consequences, contexts and contingencies. Increasingly for the past two centuries the Bible has come to be understood as a historical book, not simply because much of it is concerned with history, but above all because every aspect of it and everything in it is conditioned by history. To the extent that this is acknowledged, the Bible becomes a different book for us from what it was for Martin Luther, the Council of Trent, or John Wesley. (11, 12)

6 *The Bible in the Pulpit*, 106.

7 This movement back to the historical-critical Bible, in retrospect, had one other interesting aspect. Through the early and middle years of the twentieth century, most

seminary training in the craft of preaching itself was entrusted to persons skilled, and educated, in the arts of speech and rhetoric, rather than in theology or biblical theology. In fact, one finds descriptions of and debates about the bifurcation of theological education into the theological disciplines and the practical disciplines, such as preaching, and often the lines were firmly drawn between them. The Bible and theology stood on one side of the divide, taught by biblical scholars, and the skills of preaching stood on the other, taught by those who specialized in public speech. Some argued, in fact, that the failure of the church during those mid-century years was due, in no small part, to this cleavage. The movement to which Keck gave strong voice—and that he subsequently actualized in his years at the head of the Yale Divinity School—was to bridge that gap; but it was done in an odd way. It amounted to turning the teaching of preaching over to the theologians and biblical scholars and denigrating the arts of public speaking in the seminary curricula, something that most seminaries are only now beginning to reverse and bring back into some balance.

[8] I am aware of the complexity of the literature here, and of the important distinctions between such designations as "womanist" and "feminist." The literature is large and growing, however, and such distinctions themselves seem to be blurring. I use the feminist designation here, however, because the influence of its literature, even in homiletics, has been profound beyond what we are even able to imagine at this "close range." Only years from now will we be able, in my judgment, to look back and see how dramatically it changed things, not only for women, but also for entire intellectual streams of thought.

[9] Edited by Letty M. Russell (Philadelphia: Westminster, 1985).

[10] The flavor of this opposition is important, even though, as in every form of intellectual work, no one scholar speaks for anyone else, Margaret A. Farley writes:

> Feminists quite readily acknowledge the historical nature of human knowledge and the social nature of the interpretation of human experience. Yet feminist consciousness is experienced as an immeasurable advance over the false consciousness it replaces or the implicit consciousness it renders explicit. Scales have fallen from persons' eyes, and they cannot be put back. The fact that present insights are still partial, that present formulations of principles may change, that the meaning of principles can vary significantly from context to context—none of this changes the requirement that new understandings must be tested for truth (for accuracy and adequacy) against the reality of women's lives as revealed in women's experience. It is no fancy, no illusion, that feminists believe they bring to the interpretation of scripture. ("Feminist Consciousness and the Interpretation of Scripture," in Russell, 50)

[11] There is an odd dimension to this that needs to be noted. It is that very little of the literature of liberation theology actually discusses the Bible and its role, either theologically or sociologically. This is particularly true of Latin American liberation theology, since the Asian forms of it are strikingly different. The reason for the lack of concern with the Bible is probably because most liberation thought that originates in Latin America is Roman Catholic, so its focus is much more on the nature of the Church and papal authority. Ironically, to find direct discussion of the Bible vis-a-vis Latin liberation theology, one must turn to its homiletical writings, to its growing literature of preaching, and particularly to the voluminous output of Justo L. and Catherine Gunsalus Gonzalez.

[12] One finds this rich concept in several places in Tracy's many books, but it is most thoroughly discussed in *The Analogical Imagination: Christian Theology and the Culture of Pluralism* (New York: Crossroad, 1991).

[13] New York: Macmillan Publishing Co., a Polebridge Press Book, 1993.

[14] *Five Gospels*, 2.

[15] *Five Gospels*, 4, 5.

[16] This is the question, and the premise, that stands at the heart of Mack's groundbreaking study of Mark's gospel, *A Myth of Innocence: Mark and Christian Origins* (Philadelphia: Fortress, 1988). As Mack puts it:

> The rearrangement of this material information is made possible by a single shift in perspective on texts taken up to the analyzed. Instead of discounting the accretions of interpretation in the attempt to retrieve an authentic reminiscence of the historical Jesus, texts will be read in relation to their social settings in order to determine why it was that Jesus was reimagined in just the ways he was....The shift in perspective is required as soon as it is realized that the creative replication of the memory of Jesus took place in the interest of articulating not only how it was at the beginning, but how it was or should be at the several junctures of social history through which a memory tradition traveled. (15, 16)

[17] A later book by Mack pressed the same issues further, concentrating even more directly on the nature of the myth-making as the basis for the formation of the Christian documents. See *Who Wrote the New Testament?: The Making of the Christian Myth* (San Francisco: HarperSan Francisco, 1996), 11.

[18] Nashville: Abingdon, 1993.

[19] Leander Keck, *The Church Confident* (Nashville: Abingdon, 1993), 58. The quotation is from *Faith, Feminism and the Christ* (Philadelphia: Fortress, 1983).

[20] *Church Confident*, 61, 62. He cites Schaberg's *The Illegitimacy of Jesus: A Feminist Theological Interpretation of the Infancy Narratives* (New York: Crossroad, 1990).

[21] *Church Confident*, 60.

[22] Ibid.

[23] Ibid., 62.

[24] The first hermeneutic that Keck endorses in his Beecher lectures is the "hermeneutic of suspicion," a concept that has been in theological currency for some time, but a concept that has been utilized to describe the most radical critiques of traditional Biblical theology. What Keck does, however, is label the hermeneutic of suspicion as nothing more than the research stance undergirding good, "scientific" biblical study, i.e., historical critical method. This hermeneutic has been, he says, "fundamental in the modern historiography and so has come to govern the historical-critical study of the Bible and of the formation of Christian doctrine as well." The hermeneutic of suspicion produces, to use Keck's words, "unprejudiced...reliability of information," since this is the hermeneutic that places the burden of proof "on the evidence by requiring it to substantiate its credibility as strongly as possible" (*Church Confident*, 59). Keck, in other words, wants his own historical-critical stance toward the Bible to be identified with the "hermeneutic of suspicion." Yet that, in all honesty, simply cannot be, since the hermeneutic of suspicion is the profoundly critical stance that undergirds the emergence of these very orientations toward the Bible that Keck brutally criticizes.

²⁵ *Church Confident*, 62, 63.

²⁶ Ibid., 58.

²⁷ Ibid.

CHAPTER FIVE
Pluralism and the Text: Kenneth Burke and the Art of Symbolic Exegesis

¹ The early symbolic interactionists placed considerable emphasis on the analysis of documentary materials as a way to understand the "viewpoints" of unique social communities. Among these materials were newspapers, diaries, instruction manuals, as well as other personal and family materials. One can find this, for example, in the studies of W. I. Thomas, collected in his *On Social Organization and Social Personality* (Chicago: The University of Chicago Press, 1966).

² The problem for many contemporary scholars who know of Burke is that his work has been narrowly pigeonholed under the heading of "rhetoric," which is only one part of his enormous output of work. That designation, however, has kept many who ought to be interested in him from delving into his ideas. Thus, while Golden, Berquist, and Coleman say that "by common consent Kenneth Burke ranks as the foremost rhetorician in the twentieth century," they are quick to add that "the legacy Burke has left to communication theory and literary criticism is remarkable in its conception and execution." (See James L. Golden, Goodwin F. Berquist, and William E. Coleman, *The Rhetoric of Western Thought.* Dubuque: Kendall/Hunt, 1976, 235.) Stanley Edgar Hyman has said of Burke:

> As a systematic critic, Kenneth Burke is unique in our time, and his ambi-
> tiousness challenges Aristotle. He has developed his concepts of form as
> the psychology of the audience, of symbolic action for the poem-poet
> relation and rhetoric for the poem-audience relation, then of dramatism
> and the pentad, finally of logology and the hierarchical principle, entelechy
> and the principle of composition. At the same time, he has exemplified
> these systems and structurings in dramatistic fiction, rhetorical poems,
> entelechial aphorisms and logological orations. In changing his terms cease-
> lessly while his preoccupations remain constant, Burke resembles Picasso;
> like Picasso, Burke will probably seem to a later age to have been a syndi-
> cate. (*Terms for Order*, Bloomington: University of Indiana Press, 1964, vii.)

³ See Booth, *Critical Understanding: The Powers and Limits of Pluralism* (Chicago: University of Chicago Press, 1979), 105. Booth devotes an excellent chapter to Burke, which he calls "Kenneth Burke's Comedy: The Multiplication of Perspectives."

⁴ Burke's most complete statement of this is his essay "Semantic and Poetic Meaning," in *The Philosophy of Literary Form.* While Burke discusses both orientations to language in considerable detail, he does provide a concise statement of the argument: "The difference between the semantic ideal and the poetic ideal of moralistic interpreta-tion would, I think, come down to this: The semantic ideal would attempt to get a description by the elimination of attitude. The poetic ideal would attempt to attain a full moral act by attaining a perspective atop all the conflicts of attitude. The first would try to cut away, to abstract, all emotional factors that complicate the objective

clarity of meaning. The second would try to derive its vision from the maximum heaping up of all these emotional factors, playing them all against one another, inviting them to reinforce and contradict one another, and seeking to make this active participation itself a major ingredient of the vision" (*Philosophy of Literary Form*, 128).

5 See "Semantic and Poetic Meaning," in *Philosophy of Literary Form*, 128.

6 Booth, *Critical Understanding*, 100. Booth writes of Burke:

> There are two major kinds of critics who make this choice, and Burke's method places him with those who are primarily interested in pursuing the similarities between poetry as language and other symbolic actions, not with those who want primarily to pursue differences and to consider poetry in its unique quality. Though Burke attempts to do justice to poetry and its distinctiveness...he is really much more interested in what poetry does for poets and audiences than in what it is or how it is constructed. He seeks its special way of doing what other human actions also do. (101)

7 In the late 1960s, a movement took shape in literary criticism that began to focus on the "reader" of the text and what the reader *does with* the text. In the United States, this movement has generally been called reader response criticism, and its roots have been overwhelmingly pragmatic, that is, based in the pedagogy of reading and interpreting literature. In Europe, where its roots were largely philosophical (and more political), the term reception theory has often been used to designate it, even though, as we shall see, other more radical notions have pushed it far beyond the concept of reception. Since at least the late 1970s, the American version of reader response criticism has been finding its way into contemporary biblical studies, to the point where for many young biblical scholars this is, without question, the cutting edge of textual work. It is not coincidental that of the seven new orientations to biblical study and interpretation discussed in *The Postmodern Bible* (New Haven: Yale University Press, 1995), written by "the Bible and Culture Collective"—a group of biblical scholars—Chapter 1 is on "Reader Response Criticism." It is not difficult, at one level, to see the relationship between this reader response orientation to text and that represented by symbolic interactionist theory. On the surface, both seem to assume a very active reader and a passive text, as opposed to the much earlier source theory that presumed a passive reader and a controlling text. What we have come to, though, is an understanding that what one brings to a text shapes what one reads or discovers in the text. Thus, no two readers will read a text alike, nor will any two readers find the same meaning in a common text. Reader response theory contends that every reader brings his or her own experience to the text, so it becomes a question of: What does this text mean—*for you*? And while the reader may be said to be part of a community that can shape one's experience, still that reader has only a subjective sense of what a particular text means. At this level, the major difference between reader response theory and symbolic interactionism is that nowhere in reader response work does one find any sense of *how* one comes to a text; no sense of why one finds what one does in a text. Symbolic interactionist theory, on the other hand, provides a detailed, understandable explanation, which we have elaborated throughout this study, not only of why one finds what one does in a text, but also of why one reacts intensely to some texts, or some parts of a text, and with little emotion (as it were) to other texts or parts of texts.

8 What this means is that—as with our focus on the nature and power of the symbol itself—the "word," the individual term, is the basic element of textual data, according to Burke. Against those who would argue that the sentence is the basic unit of textual meaning, Burke and the symbolic interactionists reply with an emphatic "no"; that sentences and even paragraphs are often embedded in individual terms or symbols, whether they are purely metaphoric or not. As Burke puts it at one point: "The ideal 'atomic fact' in literary symbolism is probably the individual word.... True, a word is further reducible to smaller oral and visual particles (letters and phonemes); and as such reducibility allows for special cases of 'alchemic' transformation whereby the accident of a word's structure may surreptitiously relate it (punwise) to other words that happen to be similar in structure though 'semantically' quite different from it. But the word is the first full 'perfection' of a term. And we move from it either way as our base, either 'back' to the dissolution of meaning that threatens it by reason of its accidental punwise associates, or 'forward' to its dissolution through inclusion in a 'higher meaning,' which attains its perfection in the sentence." See *Terms for Order*, 146.

9 In *Permanence and Change*, for example, Burke writes that "far from aiming at suspended judgment, the spontaneous speech of a people is loaded with judgments. It is intensely moral—its names for objects contain the emotional overtones which give us the cues as to how we should act toward those objects. Even a word like 'automobile' will usually contain a concealed choice (it designates not merely an object, but a desirable object). Spontaneous speech is not a naming at all, but a system of attitudes, of implicit exhortations" (176, 177).

10 Booth, 107. The idea of the "terministic screen" is one of Burke's best-known concepts. Every symbol, every concept, he has argued, is a terministic screen, pressing both the attention and the emotional milieu in one direction and, at the same time, away from all of the other possible directions in which they might be channeled. Booth extends the idea to a text itself as a terministic screen; Burke would not disagree. For a full discussion of the idea of the terministic screen, see Burke, *Language as Symbolic Action*, 44–62.

11 Booth, 107.

12 See *Interpretation Theory: Discourse and the Surplus of Meaning* (Fort Worth: Texas Christian University Press, 1976), 75.

13 Burke, *The Philosophy of Literary Form*, 3.

14 Ibid., 75.

15 The idea in modern linguistics that is closest to this is probably Noam Chomsky's now widely utilized idea of "surface" and "deep" structures of language—a distinction that is at the root of virtually all "structuralist" analysis, even that done in biblical and theological circles. Chomsky devised that distinction during the late 1950s and through the 1960s. But the distinction between surface meaning and symbolic meaning (i.e., "deep," though not Burke's term) goes back to the 1930s and 1940s in Burke's literary theory and analyses. Nor is this to say, however, that the two generalizations are at all identical. They are not. Chomsky's studies are grammar studies, based on his contention that all surface structures of grammar are shaped by the rules that arise from the use of deep or kernel structures of the grammar. Burke, on the other hand, set out to work on the nature of human ideas and their formation in text and literature. It is significant, however, that both Chomsky and Burke emphasize the role

of human creativity and originality in the handling of grammar and language. For a discussion of this as it relates to Chomsky, one should consult John Lyons, *Noam Chomsky*, in the Modern Masters series, edited by Frank Kermode (New York:Viking, 1970).

[16] *Attitudes Toward History*, 237.

[17] Burke's methodological perspective is framed in various places, but one important statement goes to its heart:

> The work of every writer contains a set of implicit equations. He uses "associational clusters." And you may, by examining his work, find "what goes with what" in these clusters—what kinds of acts and images and personalities and situations go with his notions of heroism, villainy, consolation, despair, etc. And though he be perfectly conscious of the act of writing, conscious of selecting a certain kind of imagery to reinforce a certain kind of mood, etc., he cannot possibly be conscious of the interrelationships among all these equations. Afterwards, by inspecting his work "statistically," we or he may disclose by objective citation the structure of motivation operating here. There is no need to "supply" motives. The interrelationships themselves *are* the motives. For they are his *situation*; and *situation* is but another word for *motives* [Burke's emphases]. The motivation out of which he writes is synonymous with the structural way in which he puts events and values together when he writes; and however consciously he may go about such work, there is a kind of generalization about these interrelations that he could not have been conscious of, since the generalization could be made by the kind of inspection that is possible only after the completion of the work. (*Philosophy of Literary Form*, 18)

[18] *Attitudes Toward History*, 193.

[19] See this essay in Stanley Edgar Hyman (ed.), *Terms for Order* (Bloomington, Ind.: University of Indiana Press, 1964); the quotation is from 145.

CHAPTER SIX
Pluralism and the Gospel: Prophetic Otherness for the Postmodern Pulpit

[1] Cobb, "From Crisis Theology to the Post-Modern World," in *Toward A New Christianity: Readings in the Death of God Theology*, edited by Thomas J. J. Altizer (New York: Harcourt, Brace & World, 1967), 244. Up until now, virtually all of the arguments for the relativity of Christianity in a world of relative religions have been made on historical grounds, as Cobb does. What is unique about the present study, as we pointed out at the beginning, is that here the argument is made on epistemological grounds: the nature of human symbolicity itself requires the conclusion of religious relativity.

[2] John Hick and Paul F. Knitter, eds., *The Myth of Christian Uniqueness* (Maryknoll: Orbis, 1994), vii. In one intellectual area after another throughout the twentieth century, the "problem" of relativism and relativity has been faced and, in a multitude of ways, dealt with. Beginning largely in the sciences with probability theory and the famous theory of relativity, its acceptance has proceeded gradually from one domain of life and thought to another. By mid-century, the human sciences have come to terms with it under the influence of numerous brands of psychology, sociology, and

anthropology. Over the past several decades, the linguistic and literary areas of study and life have come under its sway, something that we examined in the previous chapter. Only now, in what may well be the last bastion of absolutism, religion, are we having to deal with the realities of the absolute-relative dilemma.

3 See "Definition of Man" in *Language as Symbolic Action: Essays on Life, Literature and Method* (Berkeley: University of California Press, 1966), 16, 17. This is not an easy concept to grasp in Burke, but his treatment of it is valuable. For Burke, all "transcendent" and human "longings" for transcendence are a part of the human symbolic nature. No scholar has gone farther than Burke in taking the premises of symbolic interactionist thought to their logical conclusions, and this concept is a provocative part of that undertaking.

4 A few scholars who are concerned about the emergence of pluralism are searching for some renewed sense of universalism. See, for example, David J. Krieger, *The New Universalism: Foundations for a Global Theology* (Maryknoll, N.Y.: Orbis Books, 1991). Ironically, Krieger does conclude that a new universalism is to be found in the idea of communication. The core of his viewpoint, however, draws largely on the notion of argumentation advanced by Jurgen Habermas, usually called the "universality of argumentation," or the "universality of discourse." It is a complex (in my judgment, a convoluted) contention that ultimately gets lost in its own philosophical wanderings. Near the end of his study, Krieger makes observations like this: "The communication strategy derived from the discourse of disclosure is, therefore, nothing other than the attempt to establish solidarity with the other beyond the boundaries imposed by our form of life, that is, beyond the at any time given conditions of economic, political and ideological security. Not the imposition of our myth, but the solidarity with the other at risk of 'death' is what the discourse of disclosure aims at communicating. When communication takes place within the space of the between, therefore, it must express an unlimited cosmotheandric solidarity" (157). My judgment is that some awareness of the symbolic root of all communicative activity—the unique insight of symbolic interactionist theory—would go a long way in dealing with the rootlessness of this kind of communicative thinking.

5 In the first half of this book, Mead's work was sketched in considerable detail. His discussions of these "traits" is scattered throughout that body of work.

6 All of these are discussed in detail in Burke's *Counter-Statement* (Berkeley: University of California Press, 1968, first published 1931). Burke's argument behind this is a significant one. He argues that the notion of "universal" is given its first full form in the doctrines of Plato, who "supposed certain archetypes, or pure ideas, existing in heaven, while the objects of sensuous experience were good, true, and beautiful in proportion as they exemplified the pure form or idea behind them." In Scholastic philosophy, then, "the divine forms were called universals, and the concept of a principle of individuation was employed to describe the conditions under which we could experience these divine forms." But it was the nominalists who, more than anyone, were out to disavow Plato, but so eager were they to do so, Burke says, that "they failed to discover the justice of his doctrines in essence. For we need but take his universals out of heaven and situate them in the human mind (a process begun by Kant), making them not metaphysical, but psychological." Burke adds:

> Instead of divine forms, we now have "conditions of appeal." There need not be a "divine contrast" in heaven for me to appreciate a contrast, but

there *must be* in my mind the sense of contrast. The researches of anthropologists indicate that man has "progressed" in cultural cycles which repeat themselves in essence (in form) despite the limitless variety of specific details to embody such essences, or forms. Speech, material traits (for instance, tools), art, mythology, religion, social systems, property, government, law—these are the nine "potentials" which man continually reindividuates into specific cultural channels, and which anthropologists call the "universal pattern." And when we speak of psychological universals, we mean simply that just as there is inborn in the germ-plasm of a dog the potentiality of barking, so there is inborn in the germ-plasm of man the potentiality of speech, art, mythology, and so on. And while these potentialities are continually changing their external aspects, their "individuations," they do not change in essence. (*Counter-Statement*, 48)

[7] All such human experiences are different in countless ways, even though the "experiences" that arise within the human "organism" are of the same kind. As Burke explains it, "A newborn child manifests fear at loss of physical support; but an adult may experience loss of support with pleasure, as in diving, while greatly fearing the loss of support which would be involved in his alienating the good opinion of his neighbors....Grief at deprivation is universal—yet grief at deprivation may be exemplified in lovers' partings, financial ruin, or subtle loss of self-esteem. The range of universal experiences may be lived on a mountain top, at sea, among a primitive tribe, in a salon—the modes of experience so differing in each instance that people in two different schemes of living can derive very different universal experiences from an identical event. The hypochondriac facing a soiled glove may experience a deep fear of death to which the trained soldier facing a cannon is insensitive" (*Counter-Statement*, 150).

[8] For an introduction of Levinas' work, see *The Levinas Reader*, edited by Sean Hand (Oxford: Blackwell, 1989).

[9] See Bauman, *Postmodern Ethics* (Oxford: Blackwell, 1993).

[10] An example of this is an admirable book by Paul R. Sponheim, *Faith and the Other: A Relational Theology* (Minneapolis: Fortress, 1993). It is a good and interesting exploration of the concept of "other" from a traditional (orthodox) theological viewpoint by a Lutheran theologian. But its outlook and probing differ in its fundamental premises than what is undertaken in this study. That difference, in fact, should be noted. At the end of his study, Sponheim concludes:

The other, the actual other—nature, our bodies, the other human person, God—is given to us in our living, in the experience that makes up the stuff of our existence. Thus we are not locked in our linguistic prisons, because language does depend on something other than itself: the actual experience of life together with the other. I cannot offer here a detailed prescription for the recovery of a modified or critical realism. There is much work to be done in this regard. But John B. Cobb seems to me to point in the right direction: 'In short, language does create our worlds. But it does so by highlighting features of a common world that, in its totality, is so rich and complex that no language will ever encompass it all. Different languages highlight different features. Communities order themselves to the features highlighted in their language, neglecting others. But the neglected features are still there, and they still function even when they are not thematized. When communities that have developed quite differently interact, each may learn about features of its own experience that it has neglected and thus expand its own grasp of reality' (From Cobb's paper, "Experience and Language," Center for Process Studies, Claremont). 'They still function even when they are not thematized'—Cobb's calm sentences are speaking about the dizzying and nurturing fact that, more flamboyantly ciphered, the other is given for us. Experience is given for our linguistic work of selection and ordering. (Sponheim, 172, 173)

The fundamental difference between Sponheim's study of the "other" (as well as that of most theologians) and the present one cannot be more directly stated. For Sponheim, the other is "given to us in our living," in our experience. The other is just there; and while, in a simple positivistic way, that is so, it simply misses the point of living together as "other" to "other." What matters, and matters for all the world, is not that the other is just there in our experience, but how we go about the complex process of "defining" that other as a way of behaving toward whoever (or however) he/she is. Is it "just" a semantic difference? Absolutely, unequivocally, no. It is a difference in conceptualization that issues in two remarkably different outlooks on the nature of "otherness" itself. Sponheim's quotation, from Cobb, then, tries to mitigate his viewpoint somewhat, since he seems to sense that something is wrong with it. The problem, though, and it is a problem in Cobb's work as well as Sponheim's, is that the quotation is just about language; and Cobb is quite right in saying that "no language will ever encompass" all of the elements of a rich and complex world. What the symbolic interactionists said, however, is that language is only one symbol system in the midst of a series of symbol systems from which that "rich and complex" world is made. Of course language cannot encompass it all; but language, along with other intricately devised symbol systems, does, in fact, encompass human experience in its breadth and depth quite well. We are not "prisoners" of language; but we are "prisoners" of our "symbolic worlds," the worlds through which we have no choice but to "define" and "experience" the others whose worlds impact our own and ours, theirs.

[11] See Buechner's *Telling the Truth: The Gospel as Tragedy, Comedy, and Fairy Tale* (New York: Harper & Row, 1977). See also John Killinger, "Critic's Corner: Some Novels for the Pastor's Study," *Theology Today* (July 1979).

APPENDIX
Exploring the Pluralist Sermon

[1] We are gradually beginning to realize this, even though it is still a deeply troubling thing for preachers to face. Studies are beginning to appear designed to help the preacher deal with the overt anti-Semitism of New Testament texts. See, for example, Howard Clark Kee and Irvin J. Borowsky, eds., *Removing Anti-Judaism from the Pulpit* (New York: Continuum, 1996) for a collection of insightful essays on the subject. But the problem goes far beyond just anti-Semitism, as we have tried to indicate in this book. Ironically, the best "model" for confronting the problem is in the sizable feminist literature on the Bible, the literature that describes in still-growing detail biblical texts as "texts of terror" because of the ways they enforce a particular outlook and ideology. Now, though, we are beginning to understand that, in even larger terms,

texts have "terror" in them from a pluralist point of view. For a remarkable example of this larger framework, one should read an article by Ivy George, a scholar from India, titled "From Proclamation to Presence: Toward an Asian Hermeneutic of Christian Mission" (in *JAAT: Journal of Asian and Asian American Theology*, Summer 1997, Vol. II, No. 1, 79–99). She discusses in detail the Great Commission, Matthew 28: 18–20, as a "text of terror" from a cultural point of view. She writes, in part, that

> while scholars have put up innumerable interpretations to redeem these texts toward an inclusive perspective, for me the text poses problems in terms of its christology and the dispositions it assumes about and inculcates within the 'disciples' and the 'nations.' . . . I find the texts rife with assumptions regarding the 'nation' (the 'other' for our purposes). The centrality of christology is assumed and becomes the whole pivot for Christian missiology. The 'need' of the 'heathen' is assumed without any explication. Of course there is little to learn from the 'heathens'! Most serious of all is the assumption that the eleven disciples have understood and experienced the 'reign of God' and are qualified to transport it. The whole of Matthew's gospel provides us with little reason to make any of these assumptions. Yet, these texts have provided the entire edifice for Christian mission. (89)

She concludes: "I restate that the 'Great Commission' has been, and continues to be, a text of terror for all those people who do not share the Eurocentric ideology of Christian triumphalism. As an Asian woman I wish to displace its significance from Christian theology and lament its employment in the past. . . . This is of grave importance at a time when religious nativisms and ethnic nationalisms are raiding popular discontents" (93).

Index